The

Cultural

Resources

of

Boston

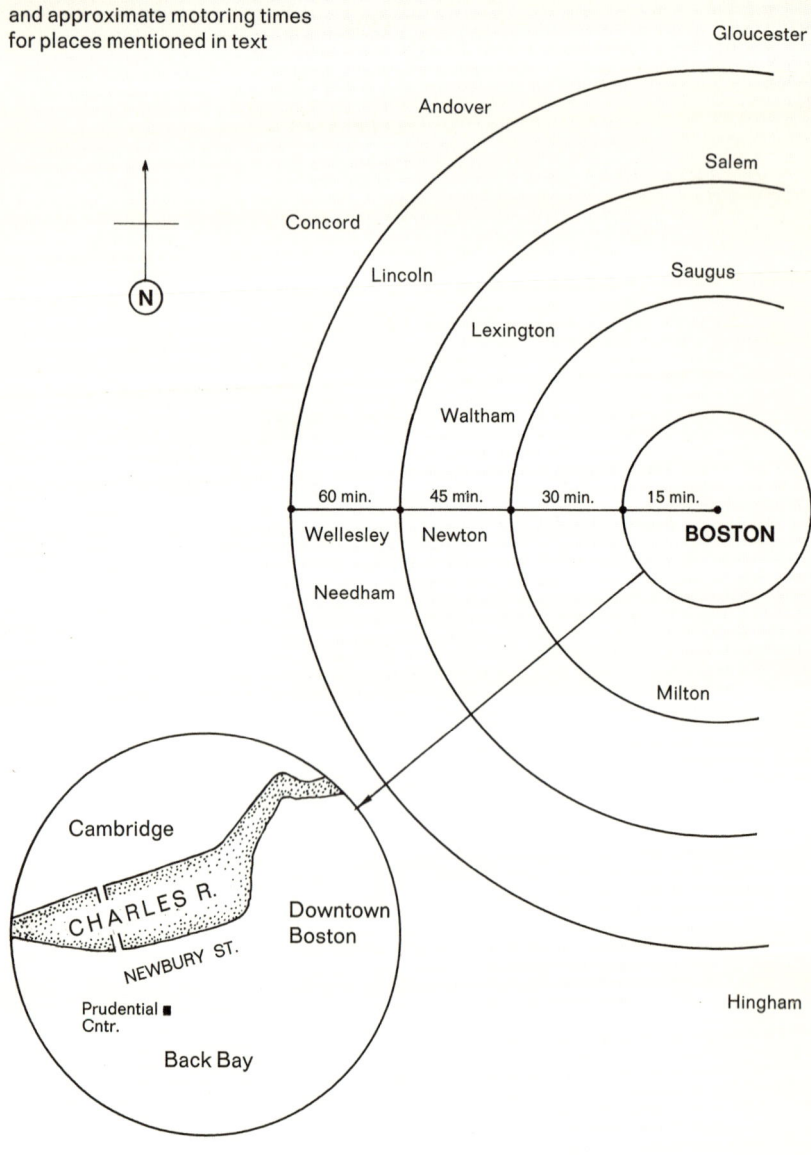

The

Cultural

Resources

of

Boston

The
American
Federation
of
Arts
New York

The
Institute
of
Contemporary
Art
Boston

Copyright © 1965 by

The American Federation of Arts

and

The Institute of Contemporary Art

Library of Congress Catalog No. 65-16641

Printed by The Meriden Gravure Co.

Meriden, Connecticut

Type set by Machine Composition Co.

Boston, Massachusetts

Designed by Carl F. Zahn

Table of Contents

	Foreword David McCord	8
1	The University Robert Taylor	15
2	Libraries and Rare Books Eleanor M. Garvey and Philip Hofer	26
3	Printing, Publishing and Graphic Design Carl F. Zahn	34
4	Art Museums Perry T. Rathbone	47
5	Contemporary Visual Arts Sue M. Thurman	61
6	Music Michael Steinberg	69
7	Drama Elliot Norton	75
8	Traditional Architecture J. Daniel Selig	85
9	Contemporary Architecture Henry A. Millon	98
10	Educational Television Hartford N. Gunn, Jr.	117
11	Science Museums Bradford Washburn	123
12	For Children	131
	Books and Background	133

Preface

It is gratifying indeed to mark the occasion of the Fifty-first Biennial Convention of The American Federation of Arts in Boston with the publication of this book, in collaboration with The Institute of Contemporary Art. Certainly it seems especially appropriate that the first in what we hope will be a series of guide books devoted to this aspect of cities in America should be concerned with the city of Boston — "the hub of the universe."

The past and present cultural achievements of Boston are remarkable; the challenges and needs of the future here, as in all our cities, are considerable. We hope that some indication of the sound base on which this future rests will be shown in the pages which follow; to those who have written them we give our grateful thanks.

ROY R. NEUBERGER
President,
The American Federation of Arts

Editors' Note

In a city as complex as Boston, and with a subject as vast as "culture", it is inevitable that a short book intended for functional and pleasant use should have to exclude many areas with which it might have been concerned. The history of Boston has been written elsewhere; her new and important role in city planning has likewise been described in other sources. Aspects of her great university complex — probably unrivalled anywhere — are described in many volumes. And there are other areas whose exploration would add to a discussion of culture — a topic basic as breathing.

We have asked our authors — all especially familiar with their fields — to be selective and critical in their presentations. All have been limited to the area within a radius of twenty-five miles from the center of the city. **Books and Background** will give the reader further material on which to base his own research and discoveries.

This is essentially a guide book, intended to lead its reader to look and experience for himself. By including articles, illustrations and listings of places, sources and events, we have hoped to give sufficient material for active participation in those institutions and occasions which give form and life to the city — her cultural resources.

Margaret Cogswell
The American Federation of Arts

Virginia Gunter
The Institute of Contemporary Art

Foreword

More than thirty-five years ago, George Blake the novelist was in Boston, and for two or three days we toured New England together. A Scot removed to London, he was by instinct and training an exceptional journalist; and in reporting his first impressions of my native city of New York, he told me that beyond its magnificent profile it did look quite temporary. The critics of Boston have never said that; and even the present dry sweep of urban renewal has not fatally damaged her ancient citadel, above which every high-rise, from the considered to the downright crude, reminds us of Excalibur upthrust, and of a basic strength not on the wane. Bad politics and dirty streets are open to attack by all of us. Few of us think we are realistic in dealing with crime. We have our share of unforgivable slums; and we have had our police strike. Along with Chicago and San Francisco, we have long since had our devastating fire. Our seaport suffers; historic islands down the harbor lie neglected. We share the cheapness characteristic of other cities. The weakest of the nation's railroads have in Boston their weakest terminals. Rich in academic theater, we are nonetheless an outpost to Broadway. But we do have certain magnificent possessions in the public and semi-public domain with some of which this book is wholly concerned.

Whatever the Athenian quality, past or present, of Boston, the visiting Spartans could always take a crack at us — and they have rarely failed to take it. Not always visiting Spartans, either. Some were and still dwell vocal in our midst. Charles Francis Adams felt that "there is no current of fresh outside life everlastingly flowing in and passing out." The fact that Boston in Dr. Holmes's day "had no second as a seat of culture" did not mean that it could not soon become anathema as well. "I hate Boston," said Lincoln Steffens. "I don't know why. . . . The general spirit is so far, far, far back that it gets on my nerves." It got to the nerves of Elmer Davis sufficiently to quote a letter published in *Harper's* (1928): "Boston is going to hang on to the ideals that built it, just as long as they can be hung on to. It may be a futile struggle but it is gallant and pathetic." If Mr. Davis (or his correspondent) was thinking of the world of John Marquand, he might also have thought of the worlds of two Boston historians: Samuel Eliot Morison and Bernard De Voto.

Now one of those ideals — a very small one, to be sure — was the so-called Lowell Fund of Boston, established in 1838 by a group of seven Harvard men, including the father of Charles William Eliot, for assisting students at Harvard College "to the benefit of many and the injury of none." To the original subscription of $11,350 *not one cent* which this handful of big

change did not earn has ever been added. Over the ensuing 127 years the Fund, under Boston trusteeship, has benefited thousands of students, including scores who became professors, college presidents, deans, lawyers, governors, judges, scholars, senators, industrial leaders, and writers (Horatio Alger among them). In 1959 the Lowell Fund was turned over to Harvard University with a value exceeding $2 million. In 1906, or 53 years earlier, H. G. Wells had written: "There broods over the real Boston an immense effect of finality. One feels in Boston, as one feels in no other part of the States, that the intellectual movement has ceased." Certainly money is no substitute for intellect; but the ability to create money and the intelligent use of what is created, as in the case of the Lowell Fund, may be counted a significant part of Mr. Wells's private achievement and resulting success.

Henry Adams came nearer to the truth about Boston when he spoke of its "peculiar and perplexing amalgam." Well, Boston, among other things, is still a peculiar and perplexing amalgam of banking, law, medicine, colleges, universities, technology, laboratories, libraries, museums, music, art, architecture, writing, publishing, and philanthropy. I think now of M.I.T., Harvard, and Boston University, in particular. For where but in Greater Boston were originated such singular notions as the telephone, the first telephone company, sonar, counter radar, the polaroid camera, the process that led to kodacolor, technicolor, the science of architectural acoustics, ether as an anesthetic agent, fractionation of blood, oxygen masks for high-altitude flying, basic contributions to the eradication of polio, vaccine for measles, synthetic quinine, synthesizing of penicillin, the first kidney (isograft) transplantation, the artificial kidney, development of blood banks, the first mitral valve operation on the heart, the art of neuro-surgery, liver-extract treatment for pernicious anemia, the determination of atomic weights, the modern computer, inertial guidance of missiles, not to mention some rather dangerous and destructive weapons? Robert Lowell writes of his Boston more than he does of my New York where he now lives; Gardner Cox has just as many portrait commissions in Washington and New York as in his Back Bay studio. The majority of America's principal museum directors were trained here across the river; one-quarter of the nation's teachers of medicine of professorial rank received most or part of their training at the Harvard Medical School and/or in affiliated Boston hospitals. And in the teaching of law, engineering, technology, architecture, and business the intellectual movement in this northeast corner was never at a greater pitch.

Beyond the name, we have the local habitation — the physical aspect of the town. I might begin by saying that to cite a city of endearing architecture and whatever charm goes with it, one does not instantly think of Liverpool. But the *Times Literary Supplement* for 28 January 1965 carried a favorable review of Quentin Hughes' *Seaport: Architecture and Townscape in Liverpool.* I quote this sentence from the anonymous reviewer: "As soon as the great nineteenth century cities realize that they have got something to show and be proud of, they will be surprised how many visitors agree. . . . Dr. Hughes [in Liverpool] looks for the best, with a genuine affection for his city but without ever over-rating." This is precisely the point. The older parts of Boston, and the better parts of what is included in Greater Boston, largely represent an eighteenth and nineteenth century city; but since when have its inhabitants suspected, in the large, that it *has* something visible to show and to be proud of? Taken one by one, its many institutions are severally aware of what they have to offer. The new Science Museum, for example, is rightly and aggressively insistent on what it can do and does for the young. Beacon Hill is banded together, however unobtrusively, to preserve its brick sidewalks, Louisburg Square, the parabolic enchantment of Mt. Vernon Street, and its look of everlastingness. But civic pride — *demonstrable civic pride* — is quite another thing. Just as the great sycamores across the river on Memorial Drive are threatened by the chain-saw and the frantic American urge to disembowel before the grafting of the newest Thruway gut, so Commonwealth Avenue — built on oyster shells and Back Bay sand — could lose its elms, the mall, magnolia trees, and all distinction of its few fine period facades for a mess of high-rise balconies and rents. The isolated voice to save these things is never the total voice. I side with all the outside critics here: as yet there is no masterful resolve to polish up the fine old Copley face as one might shine a shoe. *Tempus edax rerum:* it is a standing joke that "the Peter Bent Brigham Hospital offers the world's best medicine under the world's worst conditions." The joke applies to the whole city in varying degree. It does not apply to the Honorable John F. Collins, the present Mayor, whose viable concern with new frontiers is balanced by encouraging support of groups and individuals active on the side of preservation and the supportable doctrine of Let it Alone.

And yet one rarely has to wait for the flown-in visitor to tell you, as you avert his gaze from the beer can in the gutter and the paper on the sidewalk, what a charm and charmer ancient Boston really is! And unless you are willfully blind or prefer to live the digit life inside a glass computer somewhere else, at least a little of that charm will not escape you, even on a rainy day. I am speaking not simply of the past, but of the future of the past. Perhaps your personal errand — anybody's errand — is to see, inspect, or use some treasure which this book commends. And so you might well ask yourself — or anybody ask himself — how come it is here amid Mr. Wells's finality and not in the city where you live? Where else in America, save Boston, New York, and Washington, is there a Luxembourg as well as a Louvre? Mrs. Jack Gardner gave us ours. E. M. Forster in *The Longest Journey* says: "There is no formula in which we may sum up decent people." So with a city. Coming to Boston via New York, Pittsburgh, Oregon, and Iowa, it seems to me now a miracle that I have never lost what I should never have found elsewhere. It

would take John Betjeman of London — *First and Last Loves* — though, to make my catalogue.
In every New England mind, if you can probe it, you will find an abandoned farm. So one of the advantages of Boston to the Bostonian is the speed with which he can escape into the country. A couple of million starlings, roosting on, in, and near the lighted signs of Washington and kindred streets each night, can make it in the coldest winter dawn in fifteen minutes. And if there is no end of starlings here, there is certainly no end of *rus in urbe,* either; and the heart of Boston, centered as it is on Boston Common and the Public Garden, has its pipe line of great trees to the west; elms naturally enough, and ginkgoes farther out toward Boston College. In spring and fall the green or gold tide washes in and out; and four brief white-wall miles from Parkman's frog pond in the Common, local Audubons can mark the resting flights of warblers traveling north or heading south. What more did Thoreau ask for in escaping his rude home of shanty boards which stood him but $28.12? And as to that, what other modern city, let alone an old one, has so fine an airport of and for and to itself, not miles away on the growing edge of tomorrow.
If all these words mean anything in context, they should provide a setting for the concentrate of more important matters on the pages east of where you are at present. That setting is not easy at the moment. The late Scollay Square of displaced bums is now adrift with dust and rubble as the city government soars skyward. Out in the Back Bay the tall Prudential Tower, City of Boston War Memorial Auditorium, and all the complex of vast plaza, parking space, tunnels for rail and vehicular traffic, are nearing completion. Radios declare themselves concerned with "the new Boston." New high-rise apartments, springing up like mushrooms mixed with toadstools, alter the city's profile almost daily. Like the bands on young girls' teeth, the mechanism gleams too brightly now against the older enamel.

> In the race to renew urbanity,
> Whatever became of humanity?

But this is not primarily a Boston problem, is it? Any city that can manage to live just a little ahead of the future and not put the demolition squad to work simply to see what dandy brickfalls lie just back of the patina is not the worst place in the world to live and work in. Beyond that, where the sprawl of what we call the greater part of any city is taking us today, I do not know. Close at hand, the present blueprints for the famous finger wharves of Boston harborside would seem to promise cleanliness and taste enough. Perhaps Boston

Foreword

should have remained an island which, in the beginning, she was for all impractical purposes. Island or no, she is still with us; and the best report I can give you is in the following notes I made some years ago. New rings don't change the heart of one old tree. The sole spectacular new dimension of today is in that view from the top of the 52-story Prudential building — the tallest structure, as some anonymous wag has put it, on the U.S. mainland, granted that Manhattan lies off-shore. As it is in San Francisco blest with eminence, one can now see the symmetry, the topographical order of old Boston; her harbor full of islands; her landmarks, parks, docks, river, drumlins, bridges; the glacial bight of coastal Boston; the unrolled map of Kearsarge and Monadnock regions in New Hampshire, Ascutney and Green Mountains in Vermont, the hillside overhang of Providence. But I was saying:

I like the way that Boston leans back in brick and stone, in soot and smoke, against her diminutive hills. I like the way the old red face of her peers through the blue mist in the morning and dissolves into the dark when the sun drains out of the solvent streets. I like the slant of light at midday on the thousand chimney pots on the one hand and the smoky granite on the other. I like the white plumes of steam that issue swirling from her downtown rooftops on a cold and blowing November afternoon. I like the gentle look of rain on her doorstep. I like the deep laryngal sound of harbor whistles floating in on the cold damp easterly, just ahead of enveloping fog. I like the fellowship of church bells on a Sunday morning and the spell of chimes and carillon hymn tunes drifting north across Back Bay. I like the inexhaustible freshness of an October day and the strongest March winds that ever blew in any city east of Michigan. I like the flight of lavender windowpanes on Beacon Street and the two or three on Commonwealth, and the sudden glimpse of red and blue and yellow in the inner gardens back of unexpected windows. I like the occasional iron handrails to help the old and young down slippery streets on slippery days. I like the narrowness of streets that should be wide and the wideness of streets that might be narrow. I like the old-fashioned faded lettering on the signs of shops and warehouses leaning toward the harbor. I like the market set off by Greek New England buildings, and general bedlam, and open carts so openly arrived at, blending the exuberance of fish with the indestructibility of garlic. I like the many steps on Blackstone Street leading down by night to lighted markets underground. I like the multiple names of stores that read like the multiple names of distinguished law firms. I like the patchwork of old and honest iron and brass surviving into a century that greatly prefers a chromium front and the cheap streamline of fake obsidian.

The Cultural Resources of Boston

I like the austere slant of the Common and the contrasting level radiance of the Public Garden. I like the Public Garden's spread of trees; but always the scholar tree first.

I like the placid, imperceptible flow of the Charles — a river that somehow failed to hurry throughout history, and winds to sea from under a bridge named for Longfellow and between the Cambridge and Boston symbols for a bottle of ink and a bottle of iodine. I like, as any youngster likes, the roar of these last few trains into and out of the heart of the city, and the gleaming arteries that stretch away to Ottawa, Seattle, New Orleans, and Mexico. I like to rediscover how endlessly fascinating it is to forsake the noise and trammel and fever of Boston for the lure of the deep canyons of New York and return home pleasantly shocked by the drowsiness of a wise and shabby old village I had forgotten.

I like the people of Boston for what they were and are and will be. One has to admire the conservative quality in the dwindling handful that keeps old institutions alive, good reputations intact, and a strong idealism predominant. With the growth of the nation certain things have passed out of New England, industrial and otherwise, for you can't shift the center of gravity anywhere without displacement of its influence. Yet Boston has never lost her universal supremacy for being independent in character, original in enterprise, unwilling to follow whenever she is reasonably equipped to lead. If she has surrendered any of her intellectual heritage, she is still too occupied in serving the humanities and human beings to pause for an audit.

Industrious in industry, she has never stopped growing. Her natural conservatism has at no time interfered with generous instruction in civil liberties. She has been a proving ground for everything from invention and discovery to politics and law. She is modest. She has more visitors annually than can very well be handled, but let no one tell you that she lacks in hospitality. She has been sketched by thousands but has never had time to sit for a full-length portrait. She is an old city constantly renewed, but she has never had her face lifted — not even in the present complex hour. She is part of America, and the spiritual home of many who have never seen her rising from the sea, but whose fathers saw her as theirs before them.

DAVID McCORD

1 The University

From the days when every New England household had to give Harvard College twelvepence, or a peck of corn, or its value in unadulterated wampum peag, the importance of the university as a cultural cornerstone of Boston has been observed. The idea of culture, however, has experienced startling transformations within the last century, and, as a result, Boston's colleges are currently assuming a much broader public role which may be expected to expand even further.

To illustrate the metamorphosis, let us consider the cultural role of Harvard in 1815. Van Wyck Brooks relates that "for a thorough Boston lawyer, a merchant who desired a well-trained mind, a minister who did not indulge in raptures, Harvard proved to be an adequate nest. It fostered polite, if not beautiful letters, it sent one back to Plutarch for one's models, it sharpened the reasoning faculties, it settled one's grounds for accepting a Christian faith that always knew where to draw the line.

"In short, the college was a little realm as fixed and final as a checkerboard. All one had to do was to play the game."

Against this closed and belletristic environment, one may superimpose the contemporary evidence phrased in the harsh, conclusive language of statistics. Greater Boston contains about half the eighty-two four-year degree-granting colleges and universities of Massachusetts. The population of these campuses, including faculty and administrative personnel, is estimated in excess of 200,000. Further concentration of industries such as the electronics firms which depend upon the educational raw material probably adds another 100,000 to the total.

Thus, an intricate linkage of education and economics influences the shape of Boston's cultural resources. Certain well-defined, traditional and limited areas of undergraduate life can still be regarded as fixed and final; but if the game was once checkers, today, because of the dynamic, pluralistic tensions of society at large, it is more apt to be three-dimensional chess. The colleges no longer confine themselves to the study of culture; they actively create it.

Historically, the marketplace of American art and letters shifted from Boston to New York after the Civil War. The adjustment to a secondary position gave Boston a massive cultural inferiority complex from which it is only now recovering. The city lived on its past; the parochial present found solace in the vestigial remnants of glory such as the Boston Symphony Orchestra, the Museum of Fine Arts and Mrs. Gardner's Venetian palace. If, a hundred years ago, one could not throw a stone within a 30-mile radius of the State

House without striking a poet or a philosopher, a later pellet might have rebounded from a lobbyist or an insurance salesman.

Boston's educational institutions did little to improve the situation, not out of perversity, but out of a narrow conception of their cultural role, based more or less on the assumptions of 1815, that their function was the cultivation of the intellect — and, hopefully, character — rather than aesthetic sensibility. The experience of George Pierce Baker and his 47 Workshop for playwrights at Harvard (later at Yale) typified the approach, still resolutely pragmatic and suspicious of the unorthodox and the experimental.

In consequence, Boston stagnated, its unhappy cultural torpor increased by memory, its energies devoted to the absorption of the immigrant Irish into the Yankee cultural milieu, and its otherwise excellent educational resources devoted to the disciplines of pure reason. The universities were slow to respond. Boston was unable to establish a theater of its own; painters and sculptors of any ability gravitated toward New York and national recognition through the apparatus of mass communication centered there; letters, with a few notable exceptions, languished; only in music did the standards of old burn undiminished.

Awareness of Boston's cultural potential on the university level did not occur overnight, but when it came progress was swift. In the city itself the ancient social lines were altering, the insular consciousness changing. The Irish had long since become more Yankee than the Yankees themselves; other waves of immigration were bursting upon the shore. The pace quickened with the impact of World War II and its pressures upon the existing educational facilities; and the postwar boom and expansion brought with it different ideas of cultural purpose.

Universities now fostered poets-in-residence and visiting lecturers in the dance. Central to the new conception was the importance of the imagination and its vision, as vital as the intellect and its vision. Town-gown relationships became more closely intermingled; the idea of the college as a community asset was also undergoing a change. If the universities gave refuge to the artist with grants and scholarships and foundations, the artist's reflection of the temper of the times reached out into the surrounding territory and left its mark.

Less than ten years ago The Harvard Dramatic Society still performed on the stage of Sanders Theater, which lacked a proscenium arch, and, flanked by togaed statuary and varnished woodwork, existed in a setting that General Grant might have admired. The first Brandeis art exhibit of the same

The University

vintage was held in a building of vague Mexican-Gothic antecedents, once part of a veterinary college on the spot; and at M.I.T. there was apprehension that the extreme of specialization had been reached.

Today the problem facing the new arrival in Boston is not a lack of cultural events offered the public through the resources of the campus, but a superabundance. At M.I.T. the scope and richness of events in the humanities undoubtedly surpasses anything on a comparable level in the nation, with the possible exception of The University of California. Harvard alone possesses eight museums in Cambridge (it is interesting to note that in 1950 Harvard spent more on fine art than any U.S. university, and that today its budget is three times greater); while Brandeis is on the verge of a theatrical renaissance with an ambitious program and a playhouse of imposing proportions, or rather three stages in one, contained in the Spingold Theater Arts Center.

Concerts, lectures, art exhibits, dance programs — a dizzying multiplicity of events confronts the public. Most are free (but for free admission one must maintain close watch over the periodicals issued by the college), and the real dilemma is one of selectivity.

Harvard's museums include the Fogg, perhaps the most extensive university museum (70,000 items) in the world; the delicately-detailed Ware Collection of Glass Flowers; and the Peabody Museum of Archaeology and Ethnology, where a splendid and multifarious collection of artifacts and material concerning man's origins is sometimes displayed in haphazard profusion.

The educational function of Harvard's museums overlaps a public purpose. Many of the country's elite museum directors received their training at the Fogg, where the emphasis concerns the conservation of art. Their programs touch the public; students mount shows out of the permanent collection; and the circulating exhibits are of a high order. From time to time, in season, concerts take place in the Fogg's courtyard. Its lecture halls have played host to film societies and to such events as the first public reading by the poet, Dylan Thomas, of portions of his play *Under Milk Wood* during his last American tour, in 1953.

Next door to the 71-year-old Georgian facade of the Fogg on Quincy Street stands the one-year-old glass-and-concrete structure of the Carpenter Center for the Visual Arts, designed by Le Corbusier. The building proper, the architect's first in North America, indicates why Harvard itself constitutes a kind of museum attracting 15,000 tourists every year. Bold, dramatic, volute, the Center houses design displays while its inquiry into various fields of observation occurs in laboratory and classroom.

The new underground fine arts library between the Fogg and the Carpenter connects two aspects of art; and just down the street is a third — the Busch-Reisinger Museum, the only institution of its kind in the United States, and devoted exclusively to Germanic culture. Although the Busch-Reisinger represents, paradoxically, the changes in Harvard's cultural attitudes (during the university's early history German civilization was scorned because it suggested the Hessian hirelings of the British king), it has long been an accepted part of the scene, and its Gothic sculpture and exhibitions concerned with contemporary German schools, the Bauhaus and the Blue Rider, Kollwitz and Barlach, are stimulating and illuminative. The loft contains a small baroque organ, occasionally employed for concerts. The Museum of Comparative Zoology, and smaller exhibits by the Graduate School of Design and, irregularly, the Houghton Library, are noteworthy.

Harvard's orchestra known as The Pierian Sodality of 1808 is the oldest orchestral society in the United States and first-class in its undergraduate genre, while the Harvard Glee Club and Radcliffe Choral Society also represent a university standard, often appearing in concert with the Boston Symphony Orchestra. The house system permits frequent unusual amateur production of classics and experimental plays — the annual Lowell House opera can be singled out — and the Hasty Pudding Club show, the Gilbert and Sullivan Players and the Classics Club Latin and Greek plays supply indigenous entertainment. The university's drama is now centered around the Loeb Drama Center, which is not only the site of theater but of painting and sculpture exhibits.

The ties of Radcliffe and Harvard are so close that for all practical purposes the latter may be considered co-educational. The programs of the women's college often have wide public appeal — several years ago the premieres of two Archibald MacLeish plays occurred in Agassiz Theater — but Radcliffe maintains no official public program. For information on lectures and other events open to the public, the Harvard Gazette is the best source.

The Massachusetts Institute of Technology, by way of contrast, sponsors a multifarious public program, which chiefly makes use of the architectural resources of Eero Saarinen's domed curvilinear glass-and-brick Kresge Auditorium, and the Hayden Gallery.

In music the M.I.T. Humanities Series brings in a number of quartets and visiting artists not usually heard in concert series across the Charles River. These make use of Kresge, and so does the M.I.T. Organ Series, which

Fogg Art Museum, Harvard University

centers around an intimate Holtkamp organ. The acoustics are rather "dry" with a low reverberation time in Kresge; nevertheless, for recitals and for small ensembles, the hall must be judged as admirable.

The M.I.T. Chapel Organ series, in Saarinen's multi-purpose structure, with its striking bell tower and altar screen, the Hayden Music Library Concerts, and the playing of the undergraduate organizations, the Glee Club, Choral Society, M.I.T. Concert Band and Symphony, all are open to the visitor. The undergraduate Drama Shop presents two major productions and four evenings of one-act plays during the year; and the M.I.T. Community Players — graduate students, staff and families — mount a yearly series under professional direction.

There is also at M.I.T. a 'classic' film series and a program of guest lectures sponsored by the Lecture Series Committee. More directly concerned with the public are the art exhibits at the spacious Hayden Gallery, which contains an impressive floor space and is entered past a Dimitri Hadzi sculpture of bulbous bronze shapes and deft spatial balances.

Boston University maintains an exceedingly venturesome theater program — details can be found in the press concerning its productions — but the music programs are almost as ambitious. The Faculty Recital program is of particular significance, introducing artists of professional caliber, and the University's "Great Music" series comprises a number of lectures by eminent musicologists. The Boston University Art Gallery offers a large, active facility for staging retrospective displays of art movements and studies of notable artists in depth. Boston University is also the official sponsor of the Celebrity Series, which brings in the world's concert talents to Symphony and Jordan Halls, but this, of course, does not occur in a wholly academic context.

The cultural resources of the university in Boston proper receive vivid highlighting in the free public lectures offered by **The Lowell Institute** since 1839. The lecture has always been a fixture of the city's cultural life, and in the 19th century the "Thursday" lecture was a virtually obligatory event. Competition from radio and television has not abated the Bostonian desire for self-improvement. The Lowell Lectures are divided into free public lectures on aesthetic and social themes; and the Institute also operates a free evening school under the auspices of M.I.T.

Northeastern University's theatrical and fine arts program is relatively modest by comparison with Harvard, M.I.T. and Boston University. Still it publishes one of the most comprehensive guides to cultural events in Mass-

Combined Music Clubs Concert,
directed by Klaus Liepmann,
Massachusetts Institute of Technology

achusetts in Nucleus. The University's drama group, Silver Masque, its faculty lectures and occasional group art exhibits in its gymnasium contribute towards its place in the general artistic milieu.

Simmons, Emmanuel, Emerson and the smaller academic institutions present occasional lectures; Emerson's theatrical programs have some public interest from time to time, while **Regis** is noted in this context, chiefly for the Cardinal Spellman Philatelic Museum. The cultural scope and variety of Brandeis University, in Waltham, is infinitely greater.

Brandeis has the Goldfarb Library where a recent exhibition schedule over a few weeks listed such diversity as Yugoslav prints, Kollwitz graphics, watercolor miniatures by Strahimir, an Albert Schweitzer anniversary exhibit, *Materials for a Biography of Van Wyck Brooks,* and *Prints from Boston Printmakers.* A permanent collection of antique Chinese snuff bottles adorns Rapaporte Treasure Hall.

The Rose Art Museum is a superb institution by any standard, the building itself handsomely designed in an elegant yet restrainedly-austere contemporary manner making use of a bucolic site. The ground floor contains a pedestalled floating bronze torso by the English sculptor, Reginald Butler, suspended above a pool. Brandeis has patrons throughout the world who are interested in the development of its exciting permanent collection which they have enriched by donations ranging from 18th century panels by Watteau to Léger ceramics. The Rose Museum consistently presents some of the most stimulating, unusual and incisive art exhibits in the Boston area.

Elbert Weinberg's large bronze sculpture *Jacob Wrestling With the Angel* stands before the interdenominational Three Chapels area of Brandeis, another instance of the college as the creator, which is further borne out by the number of distinguished American composers who teach there. Berger, Copland and Bernstein have all left their mark on this campus, and if Harvard's Paine Music Library is probably the standard in the field, the Slosberg Music Center at Brandeis is undoubtedly the finest performing environment outside the music schools proper. Brandeis sponsors a contemporary music series, and during the spring is frequently the center of festivals of the arts. It was here that 'musique concrete' was introduced to the United States and the first revival of Brecht's *Three-penny Opera* in the Blitzstein version presaged a marathon off-Broadway run.

Wellesley College's large Jewett Art Museum and College Library contain choice examples of classic and medieval art; sculptures by Sansovino, Lehmbruck and Maillol; and a painting collection highlighted by Corot and

The University

Rose Art Museum, Brandeis University

The Cultural Resources of Boston

Munch. They are open when the college is in session. The performing arts are mostly a college affair, but the Chamber Music Society and other musical organizations are often augmented by professional concerts.

The Humanities Series of **Boston College,** which brings distinguished men of letters to the city, and its Young Poets series are among the cultural highlights of the Chestnut Hill campus; but there is also the collection of materials relating to the poet, Francis Thompson, and the Jesuitana and Irish collections. Other events in music and dramatics are on an undergraduate basis.

Tufts has a new Library under construction, the Cohen Arts Center and the Barnum Museum. The Tufts Arena Theater was one of the original arena stages in the United States and during the summer it features a far-ranging choice of plays, either in a student or semi-professional context. There are many open lectures.

Finally, **Pine Manor Junior College** should be mentioned, for its activities are numerous and in a category with larger institutions. The Collection of Early Keyboard Instruments in the Music Building is supplemented by the changing exhibitions of its Friends' Room, where displays of contemporary African art, of the art schools of New England and of modern sculpture can often be found, to cite recent examples.

No discussion of the cultural resources of the Boston campus would be complete without the adult education schools and extension schools fitting into the picture. Possibly preeminent is **The Cambridge Center for Adult Education,** which not only offers courses, from Italian to Gourmet Eating, but which also shows avant gardiste films and art exhibits. **The Boston Center for Adult Education;** the **Boston Architectural Center;** the multifarious Boston art schools, both day and evening; the various courses in the Museum of Fine Arts and the Museum of Science, in which they in effect become schools — all these and more would add to the cultural sum. Yet the vital question remains unanswered. Have the universities, in assuming their role as the creative bridge between the public and the artist, in fact, produced creativity?

It is too soon to tell. The emphasis on the imagination as a function of education is a recent phenomenon here. The stirrings of a Boston theater, a Boston ballet are only beginning to be heard. The universities have created the climate, however, a new climate for Boston, and who knows in what direction its winds may blow?

ROBERT TAYLOR
Boston Herald Traveler

The University

University cultural facilities and events open to the public are listed with articles about Art, Libraries, Music, Theater, Science and Books and Backgrounds with these exceptions:

Boston College
140 Commonwealth Avenue, Newton. 332-3200
Humanities Series
Young Poet series
Francis Thompson, Jesuitana and Irish Collections

Pine Manor Junior College
360 Heath Street, Brookline, after June 1965
Early Keyboard Instrument Collection
Film Series

Regis College
235 Wellesley Street, Weston. 893-1820
Cardinal Spellman Philatelic Museum

Tufts University
Medford-Somerville. 776-2100
Barnum Museum
Arena Theater
Cohen Arts Center

2 Libraries and Rare Books

Well over a hundred libraries, with a wide variety of special collections, are active in the Boston area. They range from the Boston Public Library, with over two million volumes, to small, highly specialized, and often little-known independent societies. The numerous colleges and schools in the area, led by Harvard with its ninety-one library units and more than seven million volumes, are important parts of this picture.

Perhaps best known is the **Boston Public Library,** housed at Copley Square in McKim, Mead, and White's Renaissance palace, soon to be enlarged with an addition designed by Philip Johnson. Built in 1888–1895 and decorated with murals by Puvis de Chavannes, Edwin Austin Abbey, and John Singer Sargent, its special collections include the Barton, George Ticknor, and Reverend Thomas Prince libraries, William Lloyd Garrison and other anti-slavery manuscripts, the Brown music collection, and the Albert H. Wiggin collection of 19th- and 20th-century prints, which features changing exhibitions.

Boston and New England history are emphasized in many local collections, most especially at the **Massachusetts Historical Society,** 1154 Boylston Street, with a notable collection of regional history and biography, Massachusetts imprints and manuscripts. **The Boston Athenaeum,** a large building, but still numbered as 10½ Beacon Street, is concerned not only with history, but also with literature and the fine arts, and has extensive holdings of New England colonial literature, views of Boston, early newspapers, and Confederate imprints. Special collections include the library of George Washington and the theological library sent to King's Chapel in 1698 by William III.

In the **Massachusetts Archives** in Bulfinch's gold-domed State House there are important collections of manuscripts from the Colonial, Revolutionary, and Civil War periods, plus Massachusetts broadsides, newspapers, periodicals, and books to be found in the third-floor Massachusetts State Library. In the basement-level Archives Museum are such notable items as William Bradford's 17th-century manuscript "Of Plimoth Plantation" (on loan from the State Library), the Massachusetts Bay Colony Charter granted by Charles I in 1628–29, and Paul Revere's copperplates for his prints showing the landing of British troops in Boston in 1768 and the "Boston Massacre" of 1770.

The Society for the Preservation of New England Antiquities, in the handsome 18th-century Harrison Gray Otis house at 141 Cambridge Street, has a special collection of architectural books, photographs, and measured drawings, while the **New England Historic Genealogical Society,** 101 Newbury

Houghton Library rotunda, Harvard University

Street, specializes in genealogy, family and local history.

The Museum of Fine Arts library, on Huntington Avenue, reflects the special collections for which the Museum is noted, such as Egyptian, Greek, Roman, and Asiatic art, textiles, and prints, and consists of photographs as well as reference books and periodicals. Rare books and prints are found in the Print Room.

Special collections dealing with a broad range of scientific subjects and including early imprints are at the **Museum of Science** at Science Park, the **Massachusetts Horticultural Society,** at 300 Massachusetts Avenue, with its notable collection of herbals, and, most important, at the new **Francis A. Countway Library** (scheduled to open at the end of April, 1965), near the Harvard Medical School and the Peter Bent Brigham Hospital. This last library, combining the Boston Medical Library and the Harvard Libraries of Medicine and Public Health, contains, in addition to its great modern working collection, the Oliver Wendell Holmes library, medieval and Renaissance medical manuscripts, and medical incunabula.

In Cambridge, the Harvard University collections are diversified in numerous special, research, and departmental libraries. Within the Harvard Yard are the Widener Library building, containing the bulk of the **Harvard College Library** and a memorial collection of Harry Elkins Widener's own books; the Lamont Library for undergraduates; and the Houghton Library, with special collections of both illuminated and literary manuscripts, printing and graphic arts, the theater, and a wide range of literature. There are special exhibition rooms devoted to John Keats and Emily Dickinson, the theater and ballet, and a general exhibition room for changing shows of the Houghton collections. Among the most important of the decentralized libraries at Harvard are the fine arts library in the Fogg Art Museum, the Eda Kuhn Loeb Music Library, the Arnold Arboretum (divided between the Gray Herbarium and the Horticultural Library in Jamaica Plain), the Chinese-Japanese Library of the Harvard Yenching Institute, the library of the Peabody Museum of Archaeology and Ethnology, the Baker Library and the Kress Library of the Graduate School of Business Administration, the Graduate School of Design, the Andover-Harvard Theological Library, the Law School Library, the Graduate School of Public Administration Library, and the Gordon McKay Library of Engineering and Applied Physics. In addition, the various sciences and languages and the undergraduate houses have their own study collections of books. In the **Radcliffe College Library,** the Archives are of particular interest for the study of the education of women. Although the bulk of Longfellow's books are on deposit in the Houghton Library, some of his collection is still at the **Longfellow House,** 105 Brattle Street, Cambridge.

At the Massachusetts Institute of Technology, a few miles south-east of Harvard Square in Cambridge, is another vast complex of libraries, with emphasis on science and engineering. **The Charles Hayden Memorial Library** is the headquarters of this system, which includes a library for each of the five academic schools of the Institute and two branch libraries. Especially notable are the Rotch Library of Architecture and Planning, the Theodore N. Vail collection of prints and broadsides of the early history of aeronautics, the Dewey Library of economics, the Lindgren Library of geology, the Engineering Library, and the Aeronautics and Astronautics Libraries.

Among the many **other academic collections** of books in Boston might be mentioned Boston University, 705 Commonwealth Avenue, specializing in African studies and Lincolniana, and with a rare book room devoted to the book arts, fine and early printing, contemporary literature and criticism, including manuscripts in this area; Simmons College, 300 The Fenway, with

The Boston Athenaeum

The Cultural Resources of Boston 30

Boston Public Library, courtyard

collections strong in library science, the history of social work, and nursing; the New England Conservatory of Music, 290 Huntington Avenue, with a collection of Asiatic and ancient Western instruments, illuminated music manuscripts, letters of musicians, and Debussy's holograph manuscript of "Pélleas et Mélisande."

Academic libraries of interest just **outside the city** include Boston College, in Newton, with special collections of Francis Thompson, the Meynells, Jesuitana, Jamaica and the West Indies; Brandeis University (the Goldfarb Library) in Waltham, with a large collection of Daumier prints, some of which are always on exhibition, Hebraica, and the Bern Dibner collection of Leonardo da Vinci; Wellesley College, with a rare book room containing the Plimpton collection of Italian Renaissance books and manuscripts and also specializing in the book arts, English and American poetry, and Robert and Elizabeth Barrett Browning manuscript material; the Babson Institute of Business in Wellesley, which contains Sir Isaac Newton's library, housed in a replica of the library in Newton's own London house, reconstructed with the original timbers; and the **Zion Research Library** containing rare manuscripts and Bibles.

Finally, **other libraries of interest** in the Boston area are the Robbins Library in Arlington, with a notable collection of old master prints; the Peabody Museum in Salem, whose library contains Polynesian books and imprints and material on ethnology and Pacific and Arctic voyages; the Essex Institute in Salem, specializing in the history of New England and of China and the China trade; and the Air Force Cambridge Research Library (AFCRL) at the Laurence G. Hanscom Field in Bedford, specializing in geophysics and cartography, which is one of the new outstanding libraries of the Air Force.

For further information about libraries in the Boston area and for pursuit of his own special interests, the reader is referred to the latest issue of the **American Library Directory.** Included here are the open hours of the libraries mentioned above.

ELEANOR M. GARVEY
PHILIP HOFER
Houghton Library
Harvard University

The Cultural Resources of Boston

In many of the private libraries, the use of books is restricted to members or qualified scholars, yet there are often exhibitions to which visitors are welcome. The academic libraries are on reduced schedule during vacations.

Air Force Cambridge Research Library (AFCRL)
Laurence G. Hanscom Field, Bedford
Monday – Friday, 8.15 a.m.–4.30 p.m.

Babson Institute of Business
Wellesley Hills
Newton collection open by appointment, call 235-1200

Boston Athenaeum Library
10½ Beacon Street (near State House)
Boston
Not open to the public; admission by appointment only.

Boston College Library
Newton
Monday – Friday, 9 a.m.–11 p.m.;
Saturday, 9 a.m.–5 p.m.; Sunday,
1–10 p.m. (Reading Room only)

Boston Public Library
Copley Square, Boston
Monday – Friday, 9 a.m.–9 p.m.;
Saturday, 9 a.m.–6 p.m.; Sunday,
2–6 p.m.
Print Room, Monday – Friday, 9 a.m.–5 p.m. The exhibition area is open whenever the library is.

Boston University
705 Commonwealth Avenue, Boston
Monday – Thursday, 8.30 a.m.–midnight;
Friday, 8.30 a.m.–10 p.m.; Saturday,
9 a.m.–5 p.m.; Sunday, 2–10 p.m.
The exhibition hall of the Rare Book Room is open Monday–Friday, 9 a.m.–9 p.m.

Brandeis University
Goldfarb Library
415 South Street, Waltham
Monday – Friday, 9 a.m.–5 p.m.

Francis A. Countway Library of Medicine
near Harvard Medical School and Peter Bent Brigham Hospital, Boston
Hours to be announced when new building opens

Essex Institute
132 Essex Street, Salem
Tuesday – Saturday, 9 a.m.–4.30 p.m.;
Sunday, 2–5 p.m.

Harvard University Library
Cambridge
Widener Library, Monday – Friday,
9 a.m.–10 p.m.; Saturday, 9 a.m.–5 p.m.
Houghton Library, Monday – Friday,
9 a.m.–5 p.m.; Saturday, 9 a.m.–1 p.m.
For hours of other Harvard libraries, call UN 8-7600 and ask for library in question.

Massachusetts Historical Society
1154 Boylston Street, Boston
Monday – Friday, 9 a.m.–4.45 p.m.

Massachusetts Horticultural Society
300 Massachusetts Avenue, Boston
Monday – Friday, 9 a.m.–5 p.m.

Massachusetts Institute of Technology Libraries
Memorial Drive and Massachusetts Avenue, Cambridge
Hayden Memorial Library, Monday – Friday, 8 a.m.–10.45 p.m.; Saturday,
8 a.m.–9 p.m.; Sunday, 1–10.45 p.m.
For schedules of other libraries, call 864-6900 and ask for library in question.

Massachusetts State Archives and State Library
State House, Beacon Street, Boston
Monday – Friday, 9 a.m.–5 p.m.

Libraries and Rare Books

Museum of Fine Arts
Huntington Avenue, Boston
Tuesday – Friday, 10 a.m.–4.20 p.m.;
Saturday (October–May only), 10 a.m.–
1 p.m.

Museum of Science
Science Park, Boston
Tuesday – Thursday, 10 a.m.–5 p.m.;
Friday, 10 a.m.–10 p.m.; Saturday,
10 a.m.–5 p.m.

New England Conservatory of Music
290 Huntington Avenue, Boston
Monday – Friday, 8.30 a.m.–10 p.m.;
Saturday, 9 a.m.–noon

New England Historic Genealogical Society
101 Newbury Street (near Copley Square), Boston
Monday – Friday, 9 a.m.–4.45 p.m.

Peabody Museum
East India Marine Hall, Essex Street, Salem
Monday – Saturday, 9 a.m.–5 p.m.
(November – February, 9 a.m.–4 p.m.);
Sunday, 2–5 p.m.

Radcliffe College Library
Brattle Street, Cambridge
Monday – Friday, 8.45 a.m.–11 p.m.;
Saturday, 8.45 a.m.–4.30 p.m.

Robbins Library
700 Massachusetts Avenue, Arlington
Monday – Friday, 9 a.m.–9 p.m.;
Saturday, 9 a.m.–6 p.m.

Simmons College
300 The Fenway, Boston
Monday – Friday, 9 a.m.–10 p.m.;
Saturday, 8 a.m.–6 p.m.; Sunday,
1–10 p.m.

Society for the Preservation of New England Antiquities
Harrison Gray Otis House,
141 Cambridge Street, Boston
(near new Boston government center)
Monday – Friday, 9 a.m.–4 p.m.
(Admission fifty cents)

Wellesley College Library
Wellesley
Monday – Friday, 8.15 a.m.–5.45 p.m.,
7.15–10 p.m.; Saturday, 8.30 a.m.–
5.30 p.m.; Sunday, 2.30–5.45 p.m.,
7.15–10 p.m.
Rare Book Room, Monday – Friday,
10 a.m.–noon, 2–5 p.m.

Zion Research Library
120 Seaver Street, Brookline
Tuesday – Saturday, 10 a.m.–4.30 p.m.

3 Printing, Publishing and Graphic Design

Boston printing can claim a proud tradition; the city was a center of Colonial printing. Benjamin Franklin worked here with his brother as printer of *The New England Courant* before setting out for Philadelphia. This tradition flowered in the work of Daniel Berkeley Updike, first as designer for The Riverside Press and later as proprietor of his own Merrymount Press. Bruce Rogers, Updike's successor at The Riverside Press was a kindred spirit, but moved on to New York in 1913. Updike continued to reign over Boston printing until his death in 1941, and the attempt to carry on the press without him failed. How pervasive his influence was can be seen by examining the catalogues of the Fifty Books of the Year exhibitions from 1923, its inception, until 1941.

So, printing in Boston is often considered synonymous with the names Updike and Rogers. This is at the same time its strength and its weakness. *Strength,* because they rescued American printing from the nineteenth century doldrums of shoddy materials and typographical pot-pourri, and in the same spirit quickly dispensed with the vogue of imitating William Morris's archaic style. They had an intuitive feeling for typography, and a design vocabulary based on worthy historical examples. *Weakness,* because Updike's press so monopolized private and institutional printing that after his death no competent successor emerged. His influence was so wide and his product so good that his contemporaries who have survived him are stymied by hindsight.

Updike, Rogers, Dwiggins and a few others were the forebears of a new profession (if you will) — the typographic designer. During their time, for reasons of economy, education or taste, the printer ceased to control the appearance of his product. The designer assumed this responsibility even though he did not operate the press himself. The rift has widened today as printing technology has increased and graphic design has become more specialized. Few Boston printers employ their own designers, but almost all take their directions from those of their clients.

Printing equipment and techniques, as well as clients' requirements, have changed markedly since 1941. Offset lithography has grown at the expense of letterpress printing. Good halftone engravings, monotype composition and satisfactory letterpress paper have all become more difficult to obtain. Offset printing, however, is still relatively undeveloped; the photographic materials necessary to it are too variable, and the process lacks the tactile qualities of letterpress.

In Boston there are several offset printers whose product is better than

Printing, Publishing and Graphic Design 35

average and on occasion is excellent. But the standard is low in proportion to the volume of printing produced here for New England clients and for many from other parts of the country. Plimpton Press and Murray Printing Company together account for much of the work of New York publishers. A glance through the catalogues of the Fifty Books of the Year exhibitions will show that following World War II the locus of good bookmaking shifted from Boston to the emerging university presses, and no geographic area has since dominated the selections. In these days of ease of communication and transportation, regionalism is less clearly defined and is dying. Today the Boston printer competes with the world.

Boston has always been a good market for printing. Houghton Mifflin Co. was the proving ground for both Updike and Rogers, and is one of the largest New England publishers. No one man could now design the hundreds of books published yearly by this company. Little, Brown & Co. is the other giant on the scene, and has a distinguished publishing history. D. C. Heath & Co., Ginn & Co., and Allyn & Bacon are important sources of textbooks. The quantity is impressive but with rare exceptions the product is mediocre, although this failing is not peculiar to Boston. There may be compelling economic, social or other reasons for this situation, but whatever the cause, it persists.

Perhaps the difference of purpose, or size alone of such smaller publishers as Beacon Press, Addison-Wesley, Harvard University Press, M.I.T. Press, and the museums and historical societies, make possible their better product; yet it is seldom outstanding.

"Fine Printing from Private Presses," as shown in a recent exhibition brought to Boston by the Society of Printers, represents a kind not to be found here, if one discounts that quaint remnant of nineteenth century printing, T. J. Lyons's shop. Leonard Baskin's fine Gehenna Press was never nearer than Worcester, and today is in Northampton, although some of its books are bound by Harcourt Bindery in Boston. George Lockwood, a former Baskin student, has provided a means for experimental stone lithography and work in related techniques at his Impressions Workshop on Stanhope Street, where regularly scheduled courses are offered.

What about Boston advertising agencies and their designs for printing? Perhaps they can offer visual stimulus, but it has yet to appear in the annual exhibition of the Boston Art Directors. Some excuse it by the proximity of New York, others by lack of perceptive clients. Coincidentally, art directors' salaries in the Northeast are near the bottom of the national scale, according

The Cultural Resources of Boston

A model for institutional graphics has been established through the work of **M.I.T.'s Office of Publications,** under the direction of John Mattill. The work of two of its designers, **Jacqueline Casey** (p. 36) and **Ralph Coburn** (p. 37), is shown here.

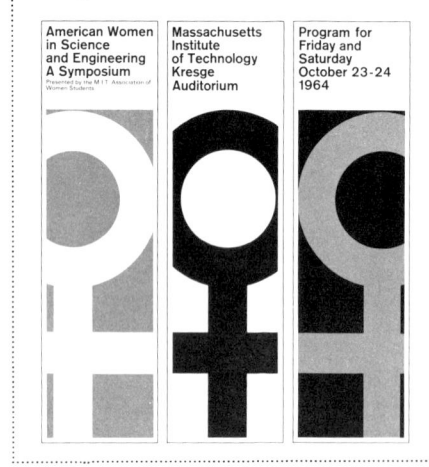

Printing, Publishing and Graphic Design

The Cultural Resources of Boston

Muriel Cooper, previously designer of the M.I.T. Office of Publications, now has her own studio in Brookline, Mass., and numbers among her clients several Boston corporations, as well as the M.I.T. Press. Illustrated are her cover for the exhibition catalogue, "Communication by Design" and a spread from "View from the Road," published by M.I.T. Press.

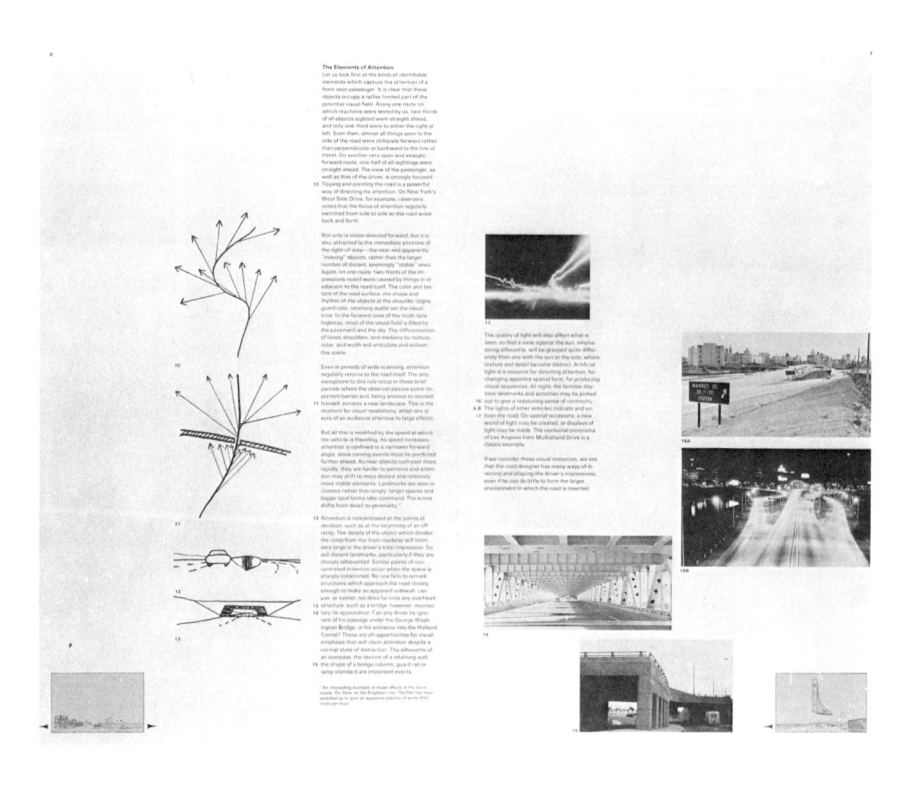

Printing, Publishing and Graphic Design

to a recent survey by *Art Direction* magazine. The average New York art director earns twice as much.

Where can we find hope in this bleak picture? The other writers in this book may provide some answers. Perhaps in the architectural resurgence on the campuses of Boston, in the bold new City Hall and the infusion of new industries. Other straws in the wind are the recent typography and design exhibitions by the Carpenter Center for the Visual Arts at Harvard and by the Institute of Contemporary Art. In connection with these events the typographer and type designer, Hermann Zapf, lectured here, and in January, 1965 the Carpenter Center held an initial seminar: "Typography: Prospects and Problems," chaired by Herbert Bayer.

Since 1957 **The Bookbuilders of Boston** have annually sponsored an exhibition, "Publishers' Choice, New England Book Show," which during the last two years has improved in focus by the jurying of publishers' choices and by the elimination of books not up to minimum good production standards. As a result, the publishers' choices have evidenced more care for design and manufacture, instead of being based on more arbitrary qualifications — such as, whose turn is it? The juried selections are exhibited in libraries throughout New England. Besides organizing the exhibition, The Bookbuilders meets regularly at its quarters at 90 Beacon Street. It also operates a workshop annually, drawing on speakers from the industry to give lectures especially prepared for new members of the book-publishing community.

Since its founding by Updike and others in 1905, **The Society of Printers** in Boston has provided a rallying point for those interested in ". . . the advancement of ideals and standards of printing . . . [and] the encouragement of the study of printing as an art . . . through publications, lectures and exhibitions." Publications have played a declining role since the halcyon days of Updike and Rogers, but exhibitions and lectures at regular meetings still afford opportunities for exchange of ideas. Ray Nash's "Printing as an Art," published by the Society in 1955, provides an interesting account of its founding and of the arts and crafts movement that led up to it.

It might reasonably be asked whether the Society has not too long dwelt on its glorious past, at the expense of losing touch with the forces which mould contemporary graphic design.

The Club of Odd Volumes surveys the graphic arts from its comfortable, nineteenth century club house at 77 Mt. Vernon Street on Beacon Hill. Founded in 1890 along the lines of The Sette of Odd Volumes in London, it

The Cultural Resources of Boston

Wood engraving by **Rudolph Ruzicka** of 77 Mt. Vernon Street, club house of the Club of Odd Volumes.

Little, Brown & Co. conducts its business from this charming Beacon Street house built in 1824.

Two views of **Communication through Typography** organized by the Carpenter Center for the Visual Arts, Harvard University, and installed by Albert Gregory of the Carpenter staff. November 1964 – January 1965.

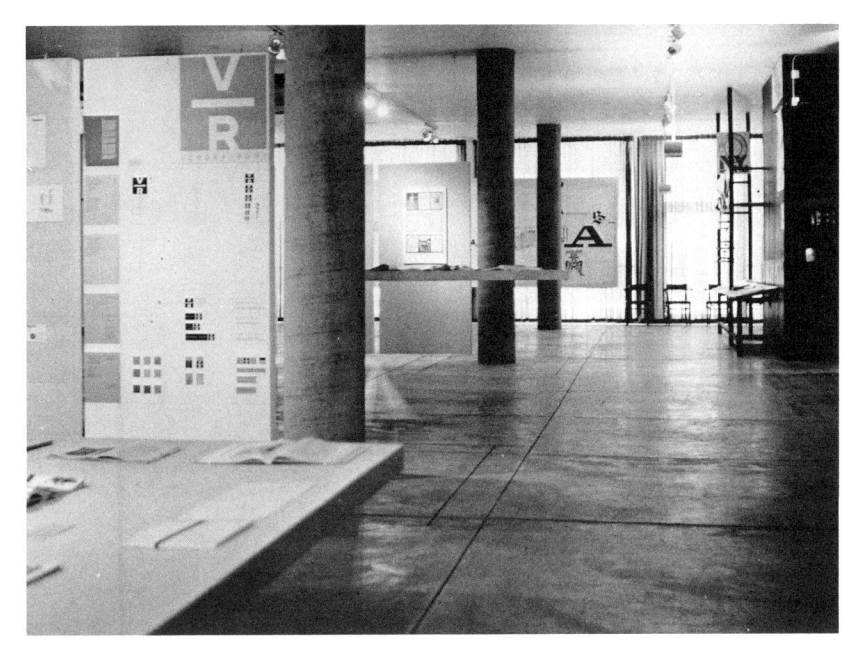

Printing, Publishing and Graphic Design

Several books from the juried selections of the **New England Book Show for 1965.**

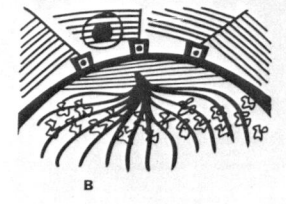

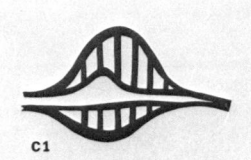

jacques
villon
villon master of graphic art
villon
villon villon
villon
villon villon
villon villon
villon
villon
villon

exists "... for the purpose of promoting literary and artistic tastes ... providing occasional exhibits ... and publishing rare prints and books relating to historical and literary matters." The purpose stated last has been admirably realized through a series of books designed by Updike, Rogers, Fred Anthoensen, and more recently by Roderick Stinehour. The current Year Book, printed in 1958 by Anthoensen of Portland Maine, is graced with a Rudolph Ruzicka woodcut, herewith reproduced, which is quite in harmony with the spirit of this club.

Despite the stated purposes of these organizations, their effect on Boston printing has been to perpetuate outdated styles unsuited to new problems and new techniques. Design has become more than well set type, covered with thick black ink, impressed deeply into fine handmade paper. The printed message is an experience for eye, hand and mind, and it can be enriched by appropriate visual aids. The challenge to the designer is to be perceptive enough to use what is appropriate, to know production techniques well enough to invent with them, and to unify the whole into a new visual experience. Design is at the core of thought expression, otherwise it is merely "styling."

We don't need a burst of private press activity, but we should expect better designed everyday printed matter from our institutions and better books from our publishers. Private corporations here have the budgets to produce effective printing, but better fees and salaries for designers are needed, as well as more discriminating buyers. As long as second rate salaries are paid, first rate designers will be rare.

For a city that labels itself the "New Boston," "Athens of America" and "Hub of the Universe!" it should not seem strange to indulge in this kind of narcissistic introspection, but it is not enough just to state the case. Words are no substitute for work, if the future of the graphic arts is to brighten.

CARL F. ZAHN

Printing, Publishing and Graphic Design

Organizations & Events

Art Directors Club of Boston
Monthly meetings for members
and guests.
Annual Exhibition, March

The Bookbuilders Workshop
90 Beacon Street, Boston
Workshop held once weekly for
individuals new to the book-publishing
industry. Fall and spring semesters.

Carpenter Center for the Visual Arts
Harvard University, Quincy Street,
Cambridge, Mass. 868-7600
Changing exhibitions in main exhibition
hall and lobby.

Club of Odd Volumes
77 Mt. Vernon St., Boston
Monthly meetings for members
and guests.

Graphic Arts Institute of New England
146 Summer Street, Boston. 542-2080
Evening courses in the graphic arts
offered in conjunction with Boston
University. Fall and spring semesters.

Impressions Workshop, Inc.
27 Stanhope St., Boston 262-0783
Beginning early April: Seven week
lecture course for print collectors and
others interested in prints.
Beginning first week of October: Print
Workshop, fifteen sessions for
printmakers.

New England Book Show
Organized by The Bookbuilders of
Boston, exhibited throughout New
England libraries.

Society of Printers
(Monthly meetings for members,
open to guests)
April: A.I.G.A. Fifty Books of the Year
exhibition.

The Cultural Resources of Boston

Museum of Fine Arts, Fenway facade

4 Art Museums

Now nearing its centennial, the **Museum of Fine Arts** long since climbed to its place as one of the leading museums of the world. As a great comprehensive museum of art, it stands second in America only to the Metropolitan. This distinction stems not only from sheer magnitude and the renowned importance of the collections, but from the Museum's long service to the cultural life of the nation and indeed of the world. In some cases these services are unique, just as the quality of certain collections is without parallel anywhere save in the countries of their origin.

The Museum was established as an independent charitable institution by the Act of Incorporation on February 4, 1870. Governed by a self-perpetuating Board of Trustees, it was created and has always been supported by private donations without any aid from public taxation. The original building stood in Copley Square. In 1909 the present building was opened and received its last major addition in 1928.

The comprehensiveness of the Museum is spelled out in the seven departments into which it is organized: Egyptian, Classical (Greek, Roman and Etruscan art), Asiatic, Decorative Arts and Sculpture of Europe and America, Textiles, Prints and Drawings, and the Department of Paintings. As a separate department in an adjacent building, the Museum operates one of the oldest and largest independent art schools in the country.

The intellectual climate of Boston gave birth to leaders in the nation's cultural growth whose names are household words. During its founding decades it was intellectual leadership in this tradition that guided the development of the Boston Museum. Woven into the history of nearly every department are the vision, influence and scholarship of such men. The Classical Department had its Edward Perry Warren; the Egyptian its George Andrew Reisner; the Textile Department its Denman W. Ross; the Asiatic its Fenollosa, Okakura and Coomaraswamy; while the Painting Department, in spite of the subsequent shifts in taste, still owes much to the underlying influence in Boston of William Morris Hunt.

Probably the first monumental works of Egyptian art to reach America were those of the New Kingdom acquired by John Lowell in Luxor in 1835. They are important sculptures in the collection today. But the glory of the Department is the superlative sculpture of the Old Kingdom, including two complete tomb chapels and the statues of Mycerinus, builder of the Third Pyramid, which were excavated by the Museum under Dr. Reisner over a period of forty years beginning in 1906. They are equalled only at Cairo. Important works of the Middle Kingdom, and from the Sudan, derived from further expeditions stand out in this comprehensive collection.

Beginning slightly earlier, the connoisseurship and acquisitive instinct of Edward Perry Warren guided the development of the Classical collection. His zeal and the following he inspired provided the Department with collections of ancient gems, coins, Greek vases and Tanagra figurines unrivalled in America and scarcely surpassed anywhere. At the same time he was instrumental in building the renowned collections of Greek and Roman sculpture and small bronzes. Greatest of these works is the so-called "Boston Throne" of the fifth century. Of world renown is the Minoan Snake Goddess of gold and ivory. These brilliant beginnings have been steadily maintained by subsequent curators for many years so that any study of Classical art in depth must include a knowledge of the Boston collection.

The Asiatic Department, embracing the cultures of China, Japan, Korea, India, Cambodia and Persia, is legendary. Altogether its treasures of sculpture, painting, bronzes, textiles and ceramics, its collection of Japanese screens and prints surpass in extent and quality any similar assemblage in the world. The foundations of the Department were laid in the late 1870's by Edward S. Morse and Ernest Fenollosa, the Yankee scholars who were the first Americans to take a serious interest in the art and culture of Japan. To their collecting activity was added the connoisseurship of the Japanese, Okakura Kakuzo, second Curator of the Department. Only slightly later Denman Ross, the scholar-collector-teacher, discovered Indian art in his pursuit of aesthetic theory and brought Dr. Ananda Coomaraswamy to the Boston Museum together with his renowned collection.

Similarly Dr. Ross in developing his theories of color and form gathered a wealth of data in historic textiles of every culture. This collection and his conviction were the motivating factors in establishing the Department. To it have been added important tapestries and rugs and many rare textiles acquired by purchase. Splendid gifts such as that of Elizabeth Day McCormick have enhanced every aspect of the Department, especially costumes, a collection in quality without equal in America. The collection comprises about 50,000 pieces of which some 2,000 are costumes.

The Department of Prints and Drawings, so far as the former category is concerned, is unexampled among American museums. Of great distinction is the collection of fifteenth century prints of Italy and Germany. Further strength in this thoroughly comprehensive collection is found in the group of chiaroscuros of the mannerist and baroque periods, prints of the nineteenth century, and American drawings of the same era.

The Department of Decorative Arts and Sculpture, displayed in forty-five galleries, is remarkable for its brilliant collection of early American furniture, silver, and period rooms — especially of New England. No less distinguished is the assemblage of English silver from the sixteenth to the eighteenth centuries and the fast growing collection of ceramics, especially English porcelains of the eighteenth century. The collections of Medieval and Renaissance art, though less extensive, are of rare quality while Boston leads the country in its recently developed collection of baroque sculpture.

The first acquisition of the Museum was an American painting. As Boston was rivalled only by Philadelphia in the eighteenth and nineteenth centuries as a center for painting, it is not surprising that the Museum collection representing this long period is of unsurpassed importance with multiple examples of Copley, Stuart, Allston, Homer and Sargent. The introduction of French painting to Boston by William Morris Hunt a century ago established a tradition of collecting the works of that school so that one of the glories of the Museum is the great series of paintings from Corot to Cézanne. Strength also lies in the Italian and the Spanish collections studded with masterworks by Duccio, Rosso, Tintoretto, Tiepolo, Canaletto, Greco and Velasquez. The northern schools are highlighted by great examples of Rogier van der Weyden, Lucas van Leyden, the "Master of St. Hippolytus," Rubens, Rembrandt and Ruysdael.

In its services, the Museum places the highest value on the scholarly publications of its staff which have long made important contributions to knowledge in every field. The Division of Education (oldest in the country) and the Sales Desk perform vital service in the dissemination of knowledge and appreciation of art, not least of these being the only full-time and fully equipped television department in the world. The Research Laboratory devoted to examination and conservation of works of art, whether owned by the Museum or not, advances scientific knowledge on the physical properties of art for the benefit of everyone. Additional conservation service — also available to others — is carried on in the Asiatic Department and the Department of Prints and Drawings.

Serving the public as well as the staff is the Library which together with the libraries of the Egyptian, Classical and Asiatic Departments, numbers about 150,000 volumes.

Some statistics: the Museum has about 800,000 visitors a year, 11,000 annual members and a staff of some 300 persons. The building covering four acres contains 152 exhibition galleries.

A stone's throw from the Museum stands the **Isabella Stewart Gardner Museum**, otherwise known as Fenway Court. Completed in 1903 to house the renowned collection of another brilliant and forceful Boston personality, Mrs. Jack Gardner, the entire Museum, conceived as a Venetian palace surrounding an inner court perpetually filled with flowers, bears the stamp of Mrs. Gardner's artistic flair and her independence. Mrs. Gardner lived until 1924, and with reason she has been called "the last romantic".

Accustomed as we are to the arrangements of works of art according to strict historical category, a scheme permitting no freedom to personal fancy, the almost defiant non-logic that underlies much of the Gardner Museum is bound to make it a unique, if not a somewhat bewildering, experience. In the long run, however, only the pedantic mind is apt to be irritated rather than intrigued by Mrs. Gardner's unconventional ideas. Obeying her instinct, giving full play to her fantasy, she created ensembles that are warm and human, if not always exactly cogent. The Museum is nothing if not personal. It therefore has the appeal of any private collection where scientific justification is no object. No one could have known better than she the charm, not to mention the challenge, of the unexpected. Perhaps her full-length hieratic portrait by Sargent in a room full of Gothic detail, stained glass, Flemish tapestries and Italian furniture is the perfect example.

The visitor to Fenway Court will not be trapped into label reading: they are minimal; rather he will find himself aesthetically absorbed by the direct and unexpected confrontation with works of art.

It must also be remembered that Mrs. Gardner was swayed by the predilections of her own era. A taste for uninhibited profusion and richness of effect prevailed in Europe and America sixty years ago. The more such profusion proclaimed the owner's familiarity with the world past and present, the better. Fenway Court is probably the supreme example of that taste, and it will outlast any others, as Mrs. Gardner ordained that nothing was ever to be changed.

The collection is dispersed through the three main floors of the Museum. Its seventeen rooms, in addition to stair halls and cloisters, are furnished more or less like a palatial dwelling suggesting the accumulation of many generations. Indeed the collection extends in time from classical antiquity to the present. But the general emphasis is upon the era of the late Gothic and early Renaissance. Paintings, tapestries, sculpture, furniture, and innumerable fragments of architectural ornament in stone, marble, wood and wrought iron are mingled in every room.

Isabella Stewart Gardner Museum,
the Court, Chrysanthemums

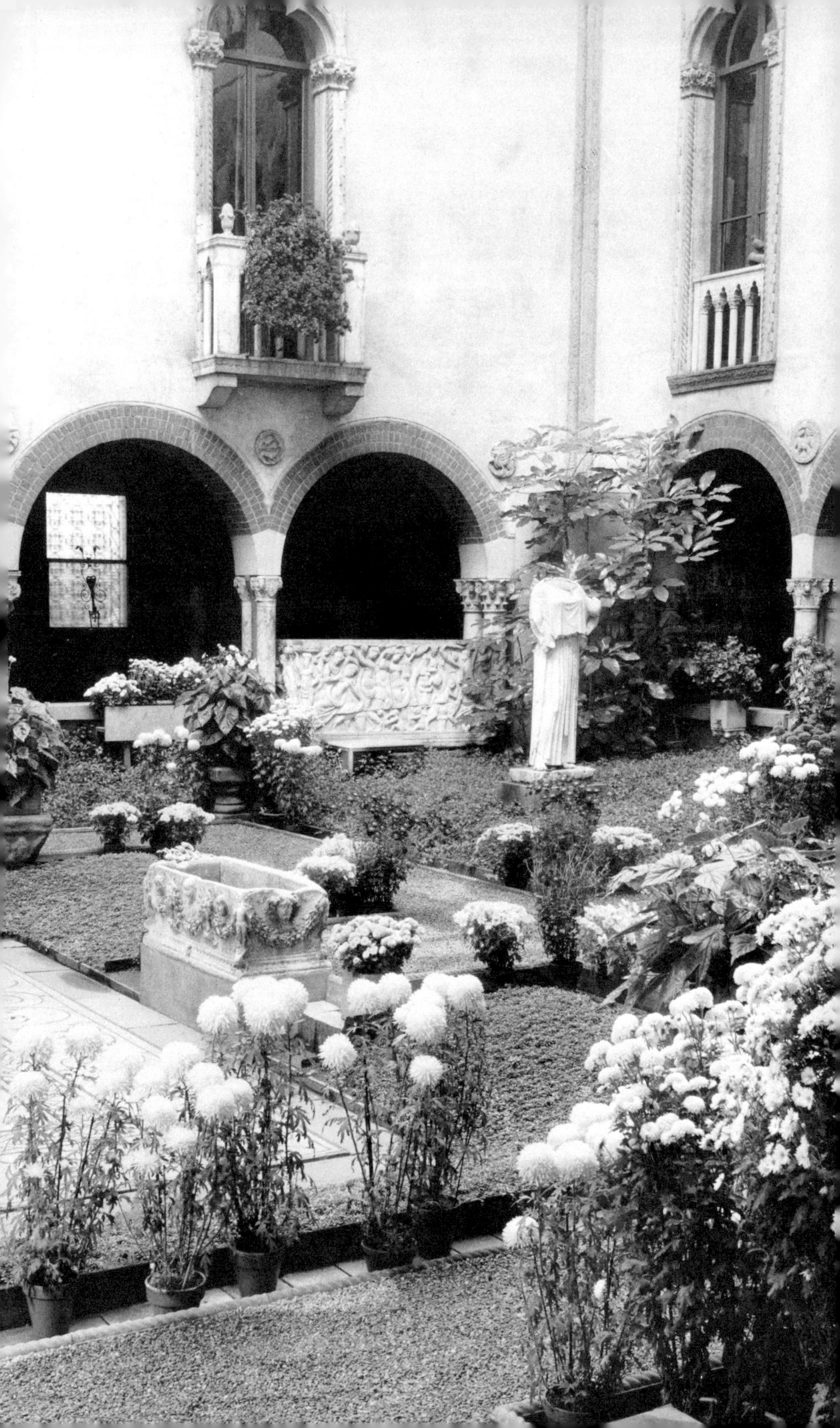

Amongst modern works are splendid paintings by Matisse, Degas, Manet and Sargent. The Italian Renaissance is exemplified by paintings by Piero della Francesca, Botticelli, Raphael, and Crivelli. Of the northern schools there is a fine group of early Rembrandts, a Rubens, and a Vermeer. The Gardner Museum also boasts one of the great Titians of the world: *The Rape of Europa* painted in 1562 for Phillip II.

Music was a passion with Mrs. Gardner. A perpetual reminder are the concerts, provided for under the terms of her will, which are presented each day the Museum is open.

The Addison Gallery at Phillips Academy, Andover, as an integral part of a secondary school, is unexampled anywhere. Given by Thomas Cochran, a former student, in memory of Mrs. Keturah Addison Cobb, the policy of the Museum restricts the permanent collection to American art. Established in 1930 and inaugurated with a distinguished collection of paintings that for ten years had been quietly in the making, the Gallery has since then made many notable additions, especially among the more advanced expressions of the present. A vigorous pursuit of its policies has made the Gallery influential not only among the students of the school, but to a much wider audience.

The collection embraces painting, sculpture, and to a lesser degree, early American decorative arts — furniture, silver, pewter and glass. Folk art is also represented, and a collection of sailing ship models recalls the important maritime background of Massachusetts. However, the works that make the deepest impression are the masterpieces by Winslow Homer *(West Wind)* and Eakins *(Portrait of Professor Rowland)* and the group of paintings by members of The Eight: Sloan, Luks, Henri, Glackens and Prendergast. Ryder, Bellows and Hopper are also to be seen in notable examples.

There is probably no livelier community center for the arts in America than the **De Cordova and Dana Museum and Park** in Lincoln. Established in 1950, under the will of Julian De Cordova, his home has been transformed into a thriving museum, beautifully situated above the shore of Sandy Pond.

A growing permanent collection of paintings, prints, drawings, water colors and sculpture, acquired through purchase and some exceptional gifts, reflects the many artistic movements of the past few decades. Works by contemporary local artists and such luminaries as Moore, Hartung, Kline, Lipchitz and Vasarely, among others, are included.

Rotating with the display of the permanent collection are travelling shows

Art Museums

Addison Gallery of American Art,
Phillips Academy

De Cordova and Dana Museum and Park, Lincoln

The Cultural Resources of Boston 54

and museum-arranged special exhibitions, devoted largely to the art of New England.

Not the least of the De Cordova activities are the courses in dance, dramatics and painting, drawing and crafts, for children and adults, and a new wing is planned for the enlargement of these educational facilities.

The Museum addresses itself primarily to the residents of the surrounding towns and countryside, but its vigorous program of exhibitions, concerts, lectures and films attract a far wider audience.

PERRY T. RATHBONE
Director
Museum of Fine Arts

The following listings have been prepared by the editors. See appropriate articles and Books and Background for descriptions of collections of institutions. Institutions are listed *by location,* proceeding outward from Boston.

Visual Arts: Institutions

Boston Public Library
Copley Square, Boston. 536-5400
Monday – Friday, 9 to 9; Saturday, 9 to 6; Sunday, 2 to 6 in winter

Institute of Contemporary Art
100 Newbury Street, Boston. 262-0600
Tuesday – Sunday, 11 to 6; Wednesday evening to 9. Closed August. Admission 25¢

Isabella Stewart Gardner Museum
280 The Fenway, Boston. 566-1401
Tuesday, Thursday, Saturday, 10 to 4 (guided tours at 11); Sunday 2 to 5. First Thursday of the month to 10 (guided tours at 7:45). Closed August. (Guided tours Monday, Wednesday, Friday, and weekdays in August, 11 and 2)

Museum of Fine Arts
465 Huntington Avenue, Boston. 267-9300
Tuesday – Saturday, 10 to 5; Sunday, 1:30 to 5:30; Tuesday evening to 10; October through May

Busch-Reisinger Museum
Harvard University. Kirkland Street and Divinity Avenue, Cambridge. 868-7600
Monday – Saturday, 9 to 5. Closed Saturday during summer

Carpenter Center for the Visual Arts
Harvard University. 19 Prescott Street, Cambridge. 868-7600
Monday – Saturday, 9 to 5; Sunday, 1 to 6

Fogg Art Museum
Harvard University. Quincy Street, Cambridge. 868-7600
Monday – Saturday, 9 to 5; Sunday, 2 to 5. Closed Saturday and Sunday during summer

Addison Gallery of American Art
Phillips Academy. Andover. 475-3403
Monday – Saturday, 9 to 5; Sunday, 2:30 to 5

Visual Arts: Institutions and Galleries

De Cordova Museum
Sandy Pond Road, Lincoln. 293-8355
Tuesday – Saturday, 10 to 5; Sunday,
2 to 5

Hammond Museum
Hesperus Avenue, Gloucester. 283-2081
July to September, Monday – Saturday.
Guided tours at 10, 11, 12 and 2;
$1.00 adults, $.65 children

Jewett Art Museum
Wellesley College. Wellesley. 235-0320
When college is in session, Monday –
Friday, 8:30 to 5; Saturday, 8:30 to 12
and 2 to 5; Sunday 2:30 to 5

Rose Art Museum
Brandeis University. Waltham. 894-6000
Monday – Sunday, 1 to 5

Visual Arts: Galleries

BOSTON

This list includes galleries in Boston and suburban communities. In such diverse galleries, the visitor will find variations in quality as well as style.
As out of town galleries have changeable schedules and Boston galleries close for some period during July and August, telephone confirmation is suggested.

NEWBURY STREET

Society of Arts and Crafts
71 Newbury Street. 266-1810
Monday – Saturday, 9 to 5.
Contemporary crafts

Castano Gallery
71 Newbury Street. 266-2132
Monday – Saturday, 9 to 5.
18th and 19th century European and American Painting and Sculpture

Sutherland Gallery
97 Newbury Street. 536-2515
Monday – Friday, 9 to 5.
Contemporary Art

Institute of Contemporary Art
100 Newbury Street. 262-0600
Tuesday – Sunday, 11 to 6; Wednesday evening to 9. Closed August. Admission 25¢. Contemporary Art exhibitions and related educational services. Art rental gallery

Ward-Nasse Gallery
118 Newbury Street. 267-3371
Tuesday – Saturday, 10 to 6.
Contemporary New England Painters and Sculptors

Swetzoff Gallery
119 Newbury Street. 536-1990
Monday – Saturday, 9:30 to 5:30.
European Master Drawings,
Contemporary American Art

Kanegis Gallery
123 Newbury Street. 267-6735
Tuesday – Saturday, 10 to 6.
Modern Masters' Drawings, Graphics
Contemporary American Art

Pace Gallery
125 Newbury Street. 262-9383
Monday – Saturday, 9 to 5.
Contemporary American and
international Art, all media

Obelisk Gallery
130 Newbury Street. 536-5432
Tuesday – Saturday, 10:30 to 5:30.
20th century Art, all media

Doll and Richards
140 Newbury Street. 266-4477
Monday – Saturday, 9 to 5.
Local and international Paintings and Watercolors

The Cultural Resources of Boston

Newbury Street

Copley Society of Boston
158 Newbury Street.   536-5049
Monday – Saturday, 10 to 5.
Representational Art in all media by Members and invited artists

Origins Art Gallery
159 Newbury Street.   267-7249
Monday – Saturday, 11 to 5:30.
Primitive and Ancient Art

Botolph Group Inc.
161 Newbury Street.   536-5862
Tuesday – Saturday, 10:30 to 5:30.
Contemporary Religious Art

Gallery Seven
161 Newbury Street.   267-0775
Tuesday – Saturday, 10:30 to 5:30.
Contemporary local artists

Guild of Boston Artists
162 Newbury Street.   536-7660
Monday – Saturday, 9 to 5.
Art by Members, all media

Boris Mirski Gallery
166 Newbury Street.   267-9186
Monday – Saturday, 9:30 to 5:30.
Contemporary American, Oriental, Primitive Art

Childs Gallery
169 Newbury Street.   266-1108
Monday – Friday, 9 to 5.
18th and 19th century English and American Paintings and Prints

Weeden Gallery
172 Newbury Street.   536-1923
Tuesday – Saturday, 11 to 5:30.
Contemporary local and international artists, all media

Visual Arts: Institutions and Galleries

Edna Hibel Gallery
175 Newbury Street.   536-9372
Monday – Saturday, 10 to 5.
Drawings and Paintings

Vanderlitz Gallery
176 Newbury Street.   262-1389
Tuesday – Saturday, 10 to 5.
Local and international artists

Shore Gallery
179 Newbury Street.   536-3439
Tuesday – Saturday, 10 to 5:30.
Contemporary and 19th century
American Art

Joan Peterson Gallery
216 Newbury Street.   262-9492
Tuesday – Saturday, 10 to 5.
Contemporary Painting, Sculpture
and Drawing

Vose Gallery
238 Newbury Street.   536-6176
Monday – Saturday, 8:30 to 5:30.
18th, 19th and early 20th century
Paintings

BOSTON AREA

Impressions Graphic Workshop
27 Stanhope Street.   262-0783
Tuesday – Saturday, 2 to 6.
Modern Masters and Contemporary
Graphics, demonstration programs

R. M. Light & Co., Inc.
190 Marlborough Street.   267-6642
By appointment.
Old Master Prints and Drawings

The Cultural Resources of Boston

Nexus Gallery
82 Charles Street.   523-8027
Monday – Saturday, 12:30 p.m. on.
Contemporary Art, all media

School of Fine and Applied Arts
Boston University
855 Commonwealth Avenue.   262-4300
Monday – Saturday, 10 to 4.
Student and Contemporary Art

School of the Museum of Fine Arts
230 The Fenway.   267-9300
Monday – Friday, 9 to 5.
Student, Alumni and special exhibits

CAMBRIDGE

Cambridge Art Association
18 Eliot Street.   876-0246
Tuesday – Saturday, 10:30 to 5;
Sunday, 2 to 6.
Members and invited Artists

Carriage House
56 Boylston Street.   547-5511
Tuesday – Saturday, 10 to 5.
20th century international Graphics

French Quarter
1210 Massachusetts Avenue.   868-7337
Tuesday – Saturday, 2 to 5.
Contemporary local and international Paintings

Gropper Art Gallery
40 Brattle Street.   354-1130
Monday – Saturday, 11 to 6.
Modern Masters and Contemporary Paintings and Graphics

Hayden Gallery
Library Building, M.I.T.   864-6900
Academic year: Monday – Friday,
10 to 5; Saturday and Sunday, 1 to 5.
Contemporary Paintings and Sculpture

Potato Printer
860 Massachusetts Avenue.   876-1850
Tuesday – Saturday, 10 to 4.
Contemporary Graphics

Paul Schuster Art Gallery
134 Mt. Auburn Street.   876-1939
Monday, 12 to 5:30;
Tuesday – Saturday, 9:30 to 5:30.
Modern Master Prints, Contemporary American Paintings, Sculpture

Edna Stebbins Gallery
3 Church Street.
(First Parish in Cambridge).   876-7772
Monday – Friday, 9 to 4:30;
Sunday, 4 to 6.
Contemporary Art

Swetzoff Gallery
111 Mt. Auburn Street.   491-3390
Monday – Saturday, 10 to 6.
19th and 20th century Drawings, Paintings

SUBURBAN COMMUNITIES

Booksmith Art Gallery
279 Harvard Street, Brookline.   566-6660
Monday – Saturday, 9:30 a.m. to 11 p.m.
Contemporary Graphics

Booksmith Art Gallery
68a Central Street, Wellesley.   237-1050
Monday – Friday, 9 a.m. to 10 p.m.;
Saturday, 9 to 6.
Contemporary Graphics

Brockton Public Library
304 Main Street, Brockton.   587-2516
Monday – Saturday, 9 to 9.
Local and National Artists

Burlington Art Gallery
Bedford Street, Burlington.   272-4462
Monday – Saturday, 10 to 5.
Paintings by local artists

Carlisle Gallery
Monument Circle, Carlisle.   369-5257
Monday – Saturday, 11 to 5.
Contemporary Paintings, Graphics

Compass Room
Grover Cronin Department Store
223 Moody Street, Waltham.   894-1000
Monday – Saturday, 9:30 to 5:30;

Boston Galleries
Show works of many periods in all media

59

The Cultural Resources of Boston

Wednesday and Friday evenings to 9:30.
Closed Christmas & Easter seasons.
Contemporary international Painting
and Sculpture

Concord Art Association
15 Lexington Road, Concord.   369-2578
Tuesday – Saturday, 11 to 5;
Sunday, 2 to 5.
April – October

Concord Free Public Library Gallery
Main Street, Concord.   369-2309
Monday – Friday, 9 to 9;
Saturday, 9 to 6.
Selected student, local and
international Artists

Gallery One
77 Main Street, Hingham.   749-5941
Tuesday – Saturday, 11 to 4.
Contemporary Artists, all media

Goldfarb Library
Brandeis University, Waltham.   894-6000
Academic year: Monday – Friday, 9 to 5.
Graphics, Rare Books

Lexington Arts and Crafts Society
130 Waltham Street, Lexington.
862-9696
Changeable. Monday, Tuesday, 10 to 2,
7 to 10; Saturday, 10 to 2:30;
Sunday, 3:30 to 5:30.
Exhibitions by Member Guilds

Malden Public Library
36 Salem Street, Malden.   324-0218
Monday – Saturday, 9 to 9.
American and European Art, local
Artists

Marblehead Art Association
8 Hooper Street, Marblehead.   631-2608
Monday – Sunday, 2 to 5.
Members and invited Artists

Newton College of the Sacred Heart
885 Centre Street, Newton.   332-6700
During academic year
Monday – Saturday, 9 to 9, Sunday,
9 to 5. Exhibitions of Contemporary Art.

Pine Manor Junior College
360 Heath Street, Brookline,
(after June 1965) 235-3010
Monday – Sunday, 2 to 5.
Visual Arts related to the curriculum

Robbins Library
700 Massachusetts Avenue, Arlington.
643-0026
Monday – Friday, 9 to 9;
Saturday, 9 to 6.
Collection of Prints: European and
American Portraits,
Local artists, all media

Winchester Public Library
80 Washington Street, Winchester.
729-3770
Monday – Saturday, 10 to 9.
Winchester Art Association Exhibitions.
During the summer, Art of the public
schools

Seasonal Exhibitions

Boston Arts Festival
held at Boston Public Garden
June – July. Juried exhibition of all
media, submitted by New England
Artists

Boston Printmakers
held at Boston Museum of Fine Arts
January – February. Exhibition of prints
by Members and invited Artist

Boston Society of Watercolor Painters
held at Boston Museum of Fine Arts
March – April. Exhibitions of paintings
by Members

New England Art Today
held at Northeastern University
April – May, Biennial (odd years).
Painting and Sculpture.
Juried invitational exhibition sponsored
by New England Contemporary
Artists Inc.

5 Contemporary Visual Arts

The Institute of Contemporary Art's main contribution to this guide has been to serve as its Boston co-publisher.

As Director of I.C.A., my own specific assignment is to "describe the contemporary art scene around Boston" with the exception of activities on campuses and in standard art museums, both of which are covered elsewhere. My focus is therefore upon that which exists *for*, and *in the midst of* the general public, and is available most of the time.

For guide purposes, we must very nearly exclude the real principals of the art scene: the artists themselves. Most artists value privacy for production, and hence are not generally available — though purposeful appointments can of course be arranged (with the Institute's assistance, if desired).

The situation today for artists in this vicinity can be described here only in the most general terms. First, our mailing files (which undoubtedly are far from complete) now list over five hundred active professional artists whose metropolitan center is Boston. Their addresses are necessarily undergoing much revision nowadays, as Redevelopment demolition takes its toll of skylighted lofts in low-rental districts. Though shifting their neighborhoods of concentration, artists are still at work all around the city and beyond it: on the Cape, along the South and North Shores including Maine, and in the interior hills of western Massachusetts, New Hampshire, and to some extent Vermont. The majority of artists throughout the area are native to New England. Others came for schooling and stayed on. And an extreme minority were brought in from other regions to hold professional assignments — actually, there may be more European-born appointees than native Americans from elsewhere. In any case, the turnover in campus teaching positions is quite limited, with the result that many Boston artists must support themselves partially by private teaching or by non-art jobs.

The overall Boston scene, as of this date, does not reflect widespread consideration of artists. Their attitude is presently one of hopeful anticipation.

Hereafter, my comments will concentrate upon two public realms: that of the artists' representatives (the **art dealer/art collector** complexity) and that of our own educationally-slanted center, the **Institute of Contemporary Art.** Whatever may be said of the broad differences between the two kinds of operations being discussed, or of closer kinships for each in other directions (the dealers to other commercial endeavors, and the Institute to other art institutions), I feel that many common bonds exist, and that it is both interesting and valid to examine them together, for once, as the man-on-the-street's art scene.

Although the combination I have described above today comprises one of three rings in the contemporary art show around Boston, just a few years back it would have been the *only* one. (None of the contemporary art interests now shown by the universities and by the general art museums were in evidence a decade ago.) And even *this* category would have been fairly underdeveloped a while back.

Some readers will remember the genuine excitement of, for example, the early fifties — insofar as the art then beginning to be produced. Wasn't that excitement mostly among artists and workers in the art field? The records prove that Boston's faithfuls were working in behalf of the art of those days with vigor matching the best exerted today. They exhibited, they reviewed, they lectured endlessly: all in an effort to alert the public to the fact that *art was happening* all around, a dramatically new kind of art. They insisted that knowing current art and claiming it as a part of one's own time was surely as important as treasuring the time-sifted creativity of past artists. The very astute pointed out to their fellow Bostonians that a respect for the present adds depth to one's respect for the past.

Despite all — just a few years back, in this province as in most others — art without accolades acquired none by being made available to the local public. From all reports, those organizations which took chances artistically were tossed by heavy seas. The best-built vessels, with the most determined crews and the most plentiful reserves, managed to survive season upon season. The others didn't.

No one seems to have noticed exactly when or how all of us got from there to here. Everyone remembers the really uphill efforts which adventurous art projects endured: the lost leases, moves, reorganizations, renamings — even closings. But somehow, viewed in reverse from the mid-sixties, the past decade's net effects are expansion and improvement.

So, the big scene is changing and the Boston scene is changing with it. And the metamorphosis has affected the older avant-garde, still centered in the Back Bay, as surely as it has developed splendid and widespread new branches elsewhere. Can our situation perhaps reassure those who bemoan today's mushrooming ART ESTABLISHMENTS? (The phrase is Harold Rosenberg's, for a recent issue of *Esquire*.) These events were altogether innocent and surely uncontrived. The ANTIARTESTABLISHMENTARIANS (our term) *must* hear this, and from a non-Bostonian: in many cases the very same individuals now working in behalf of contemporary art and artists were

Institute of Contemporary Art, members viewing the exhibition, Corporations Collect

The Art Rental Gallery, Institute of Contemporary Art

The Cultural Resources of Boston

doing so before 1950, and their methods continue to adapt to the times. Some of the "old-timers" are still not countable in New York but remain in Boston! All continue to be surprised that the going is no harder than it is today. That public visitors no longer apologize for coming in to look. That most people are here not to meet a friend but to see the exhibition, and that they usually know *what* exhibition. Finally, that other types of leaders in the community are beginning to recognize this piece of the art field. We now appear regularly on panel discussions, civic committees — even roadmaps. So much for our acceptance in Boston, as agencies of the present.

Now, does it follow that, given more peaceful waters, our ships are finally coming in — to a jubilant port, or to a lively art market? And how does it all compare with the contemporary scene in the outside world?

Even as Boston today is not living by its conservative image of yesterday, neither is it taking to contemporary art at a level comparable to New York or Los Angeles. Perhaps Boston's interest in today's art compares with Washington's and Chicago's. The three cities seem to be in step, give or take a few beats. All three are now giving attention both to the artists of their own areas and to those of the New York and international scenes, and with far less self-consciousness about them as separate creative tribes. Could some graduate student searching for a thesis topic determine what factors have produced this new awareness? Is it the step-up in mass media communications alone? Is it the added effect of the commuter routes, which are now travelled heavily between the cities named and New York? Whatever it is, the same influences relative to Los Angeles may be changing San Francisco in similar ways. The latter would seem to be our West Coast counterpart.

Why do I disassociate Buffalo, Minneapolis, and Utica as Boston's artscene sisters? Because they are taking an entirely different approach towards our mutual endeavors. These cities, unlike those named previously, have built spectacular contemporary galleries and are filling them with major institutional collections of contemporary art, using purchase funds which are in themselves direct gifts and bequests of very generous families: essentially one per museum. Their efforts are consolidative. They are not dependent upon, nor have they resulted in, extensive art acquisitional activity throughout each community. The opposite applies to Boston, and to Washington, Chicago, and San Francisco. In these cities it seems to work best to operate in terms of developing private-collector interest, and in turn to funnel the holdings — as they become historic — into the existing network of curatorial institutions. The distinction seems to be partly philosophical and partly economic.

Contemporary Visual Arts

Immediate presentation, exemplified by
new Warhol and Segal, shown at
Institute of Contemporary Art

The Cultural Resources of Boston

In Boston today we have no *main* patron of contemporary art. We have instead several dozen benefactors who can be relied upon to give moderately large sums annually to their contemporary art "charities" — for example, to lay a base of annual support for I.C.A. — and also to spend, with our fullest enthusiasm, much larger amounts in privately acquiring contemporary art works. It would be interesting to see what could happen in Boston at this particular stage of events if these two approaches were suddenly combined.

What are collectors like in Boston? "Like Bostonians": which is to say that there is really no pattern. But there do at least seem to be groupings or territorial "franchises." Naturally, some support the better known New England artists almost exclusively. Others are attracted mostly to the very new or very daring, whatever the source. Still others approach the matter more methodically, and collect in terms of movements and examples. Just as no single patron is today underwriting Boston's look at contemporary art, so no unforgettably impulsive collector is active here now. I am thinking of the kind who buys uninhibitedly and unlimitedly.

So there are creditable, useful private collections in Boston-area homes today — collections well worth seeing, if not actually monumental. One supposes that several may develop into truly major collections. They have long since passed the level of decorative needs, and have already begun to trade good for better.

As a relative newcomer to the contemporary art scene here in Boston, I yearn most of all — throughout every aspect under consideration — to see the good *passives* — tolerance and goodwill, which are definitely with us now — move on to the good *actives* — identification, impulse, impact. Every recent experiment in this direction, such as aggression and open salesmanship on the part of formerly quiet dealers, and unabashed message-spreading on the part of once-tranquil institutions such as ours, has paid off to a noticeable degree in seeing basic purposes accomplished.

For better or for worse, good paintings sell better at good parties than at dull ones, and good educational programming transmits more when used more. I doubt that there is anything to be regretted in any city about seeking and getting the fullest possible response.

If the local art market can for a time be philosophical about the fact that Boston's buying simply will not confine itself to Boston, perhaps local collectors will meantime finish overcoming the preference they once felt for buying out of town — the very same object! Visitors to Boston are probably more aware than ourselves of those overlaps between Boston and New York. Many comment to the Institute staff about their surprise at finding such high quality and broad geographic range along Newbury Street.

Boston, 1965: a place and time ripe for open-minded, warm-hearted looking and listening, by natives and newcomers alike. The Institute of Contemporary Art, which is itself so accessible to everyone's home or hotel that a detailed description of it does not seem necessary herein, offers itself as the community's constant contemporary guide. It presents major exhibitions, operates projects which encourage private and corporate collecting, schedules audience events which explore problems and barriers, conducts changing tours throughout the region, and undertakes countless other special projects as opportunities arise — for example, the publication of this guidebook.

As always since 1936, all activities of the Institute are available to every interested visitor, sometimes with a nominal cost-sharing charge to non-Members. Details of Institute events and other contemporary art activities throughout the Boston area may always be had by consulting our community bulletin board located just inside the I.C.A. entrance.

Finally, more important than all the measurable components — the active contemporary centers, the growing public response, the increasing trend towards collecting, and all the rest — is the central aspect with which this article began: the creative climate. *Is* Boston going to be a great place in which to live and work as an artist? Again, those all-important factors: exuberance and verve. Artists will be the most likely to sense their presence or absence accurately. Indeed, their own zest for fertile coexistence as creative individuals — not as isolated affiliates of *this* art faculty or *that* art gallery — will have much to do with contributing to a balmier creative climate, one likely to nourish the contemporary art scene in Boston.

SUE M. THURMAN
Director
Institute of Contemporary Art

The Cultural Resources of Boston

Erich Leinsdorf conducts the Boston Symphony Orchestra

6 Music

Boston is universally and properly known as a center of musical culture. It owes its fame in this field more than anything to the Boston Symphony Orchestra. Locally, too, that organization looms larger in the minds of the musical public than any other. One result is that Bostonians are apt to be surprised when it is pointed out how varied and how alive musical activities are here.

At the center, in musical fame, and in social significance as well, stands "Symphony." In Symphony Hall, the orchestra has an acoustically wonderful home, and one, though it is not so comfortable as more modern halls, that is a handsome and gracious place. Though the words "Boston Symphony" are no longer peculiarly synonymous with dazzling orchestral execution as they once were, the orchestra is still obviously one of the country's, and the world's, great ones.

Erich Leinsdorf is now in his third season as Music Director, as immediate successor to Charles Munch, and more remotely to Serge Koussevitzky, Pierre Monteux, and Karl Muck, among others. There are those who miss the sheer nervous excitement of Munch; there are many more who value Leinsdorf's work for its clarity. On the whole, he offers perhaps the most interesting programs of any director of a major orchestra. He is a man full of ideas, and it is likely that under his guidance the Berkshire Music Center, the Symphony's summer home at Tanglewood, will blossom into new, useful, and imaginative life.

The Boston Symphony is parent to two chamber music organizations. That is, many of the Symphony players participate in smaller ensembles in the Boston area, but there are two that the Orchestra recognizes as legitimate offspring and which are allowed to use its jealously guarded name. One is the Boston Symphony String Quartet, formerly the Nova Arte, and then as now Quartet in residence at the New England Conservatory; the other is the Boston Symphony Chamber Players, made up of a dozen of the orchestra's principals, and now in its first season of concerts.

A very special pendant to the Boston Symphony is the Boston Pops (whose European records still carry the solemn label of "Boston Promenade Orchestra"). This is actually the Boston Symphony minus its first desk players. Its conductor is Arthur Fiedler, beloved, endlessly energetic at 70, and in his fourth decade of his devoted and imaginative labor of somehow bringing "Lawrence of Arabia" into a harmonious relationship with Mozart and Bartok. Fiedler is still associated with the Esplanade concerts, which carry many of the Pops players and some freelancers to the Hatch Shell on the banks of the Charles for free concerts attended by many thousands in the early weeks of summer. Often on the podium at Pops and the Esplanade is Harry Ellis Dickson, a Symphony violinist, who also does successful children's concerts on a high level (an all-Stravinsky program earlier this season).

Other organizations contribute to Boston orchestral life. There is the newly revived Women's Symphony, which, it is hoped, will be able to carry the burden of summer music after the Symphony players have moved to Tanglewood. And in the Cambridge Festival Orchestra, there is a free-lance orchestra of good potential. There is, of course, a large number of local community and civic orchestras. Then, something special is represented by the nearly 200 teenagers who make up the two Greater Boston Youth Symphony Orchestras. The senior of these has played in Carnegie Hall and at the White House.

Resident chamber groups include those affiliated with the Boston Symphony and already mentioned; also the Fine Arts Wind Quintet, which stands in a similar relation to the Cambridge Festival Orchestra.

There are good schools in the area. Outstanding among them is the New England Conservatory, whose activities are about to be expanded to include a summer session at Castle Hill, Ipswich. Very recently its concerts, particularly those of the Orchestra under the enterprising Frederik Prausnitz, have become an important means of making Boston acquainted with new music. Included in the current season's programs, for example, are Stockhausen's "Gruppen" (first U.S. performance), Krenek's "Kette, Kreis und Spiegel" (conducted by the composer), and the Stefan Wolpe Symphony. The Longy School of Music in Cambridge is a fine institution. There is also the Boston Conservatory.

Many of the colleges and universities in the area have outstanding music departments, Harvard and Radcliffe, Brandeis, Boston University, Wellesley, among them. There is a lot of performance at some of these places from which the whole community benefits: Brandeis, for instance, has unusually interesting chamber concerts (Robert Koff, Eugene Lehner, Madeline Foley, are among the players involved), Boston University has a good opera department. The universities are centers of scholarship, and musicologists of imposing accomplishment live and work in and around Boston, including Nino Pirrotta and John Ward at Harvard, Kenneth Levy at Brandeis.

Libraries accompany learning. The music library at Harvard is notable, but an extremely impressive collection belongs to the city itself, for the Boston

Music 71

Chorus Pro Musica with orchestra
Alfred Nash Patterson conducting a
performance of Bach's B Minor Mass
in Symphony Hall

Public Library has one of the best music divisions in the country. The concert life of the city brings, as to every other metropolitan center, visits from orchestras, ensembles, and soloists from all over the world. Such events are generally well attended and well applauded. To the more sophisticated public they are of limited interest. Most of the concerts are given by the most familiar "celebrities," and the programs are almost as predictable as the lists of artists, and deplorably duplicative. The Morning Musicales, which used to be a series of some distinction, offers a kind of "celebrity series" on an extremely low level of sophistication, and these events are of more social significance than musical. More distinguished series of this kind are offered at M.I.T. and by the Mason Foundation in Cambridge.

The Boston Opera Association makes the heroic financial effort each year to bring the Metropolitan Opera for a week's visit. This, too, is a social as well as an artistic event. The musical offerings vary as they do in the company's own house in New York from great distinction to shambles.

But in opera some of the most exciting performances anywhere in America are those propelled into being by the imaginative energies of Sarah Caldwell, artistic director of the Boston Opera. Handicapped not only financially, but also by lack of an appropriate theater, the company has nonetheless achieved the extraordinary. Past triumphs included Bellini's "I Puritani" with Joan Sutherland; also Berg's "Lulu", whose staging helped right a long-standing musical and dramatic injustice. The current season's repertory includes Rossini's "Semiramide," as a vehicle for Sutherland and with Marilyn Horne; the first American production of Luigi Nono's "Intolleranza"; the original score of "Boris Godunov." The Boston Opera represents Boston musical life at its best. It is not merely that the artistic level is high, but that everything is freshly considered. It is something uniquely ours, not a carbon copy or a smudgy facsimile of opera as given elsewhere.

Boston is a city rich in choruses. The Chorus pro Musica, largely professional, has become outstanding under the vigorous and imaginative leadership of Alfred Nash Patterson. The Lexington Choral Society has a reputation as a superb amateur group; the Handel and Haydn Society is the most venerable of Boston's musical institutions. Good choral work emanates from the schools, Harvard – Radcliffe (Elliot Forbes), the New England Conservatory (Lorna Cooke de Varon), M.I.T. (Klaus Liepmann), among them. Here is another area where the approach to repertory is sometimes inclined to be timid.

Not least, there is the stimulating presence of composers. Among those in Boston are Arthur Berger, Robert Cogan (who bears much responsibility for

Music

Boston Opera, Joan Sutherland in *Semiramide*

Camerata of the Museum of Fine Arts
Concert at Brandeis University

The Cultural Resources of Boston

the lively atmosphere at the New England Conservatory), Mabel Daniels, Pozzi Escot, Leon Kirchner (who teaches at Harvard and who has made beautiful contributions as conductor and pianist also), Daniel Pinkham, Gardner Read, and Harold Shapero. Add to the list for this spring Ernst Krenek, Visiting Professor at Brandeis.

Boston is rich in music. There is not only that offered by its most famous institutions in the famous halls, but less expected places like the Isabella Stewart Gardner Museum, the Museum of Fine Arts, some of the churches, the tiny Club 47 in Cambridge, are the homes of what often turn out to be remarkable and treasurable occasions. Boston hardly knows itself what it has. For the musician it is a wonderful place to live and work.

MICHAEL STEINBERG
Music Critic
Boston Globe

Boston Conservatory
26 Fenway, Boston.   536-1574

Hatch Shell
(free summer concerts, Boston Pops, etc.) The Esplanade

Longy School of Music
1 Follen St., Cambridge.   876-0956

Mason Music Foundation, Inc.
59 Fayerweather St., Cambridge.
354-3856

New England Conservatory
290 Huntington Avenue, Boston.
536-8660

Symphony Hall
251 Huntington Avenue, Boston.
266-1492

Universities

Boston University
755 Commonwealth Ave., Boston.
262-4300

Brandeis University
415 South St., Waltham.   894-6000

Harvard University
Cambridge.   868-7600

Massachusetts Institute of Technology
77 Massachusetts Avenue, Cambridge.
864-6900

Other Concerts given at:

Churches

Club 47
47 Palmer Street, Cambridge.   864-3266

Isabella Stewart Gardner Museum
280 The Fenway, Boston.   566-1401

Museum of Fine Arts (Camerata)
465 Huntington Ave., Boston.   267-9300

Choral Groups

Cantata Singers
64 Marlborough Street, Boston

Chorus pro Musica
645 Boylston Street, Boston.   267-7442

Harvard-Radcliffe
(see above)

Lexington Choral Society

Massachusetts Institute of Technology
(see above)

New England Conservatory
(see above)

7 Drama

Theatrically, at this time in its history, Boston is a Tryout Town. Most of the plays and musical shows presented here are created solely to please future audiences in New York and are offered to ours only in transit, during a long process of preparation, unrevised and unperfected.

In Boston, while our playgoers pay to watch, plays are almost invariably pruned, rewritten, occasionally recast: actors or actresses are fired and replaced. Settings, songs, entire scenes are cropped and others substituted. Not until the two or three final performances, and not always then, do Boston's partisans of the drama have an opportunity to see and hear these new productions in final form, as they will be exhibited to the first-nighters of New York.

This grievous system, which makes guinea pigs of our audiences, is now being imitated in England, but is otherwise unique in the world. It had its tentative beginnings just before the turn of the century; since the twenties it has been almost universally accepted by American play producers, who use not only Boston but also New Haven, Baltimore, Wilmington, Philadelphia, Washington and (in the last five years) Detroit and Toronto, as living laboratories in which to test, assay and reconstruct their new works before submitting them to New Yorkers, who will pass final, definitive judgment.

The root of this evil is economic. Only in New York are there enough potential playgoers to pay the production costs of plays, which now run to a minimum of $150,000 and may carry a weekly expense of $40,000 and to make possible, over and above that, a profit. Success on Broadway can make the investors rich: failure is invariably catastrophic, and there is nothing in between. Show Business is now a Big Gamble. New Yorkers, though their taste may be questionable, are fussy. They know what they want on the stage, and they won't accept productions that are faulty in their kind, or unperfected. They want them slick, swift and perfect; everything else they reject, coldly.

In a reasonable world, with unlimited time for preparation, the producers might be able to find and eliminate most of the errors in new productions during rehearsals, without presenting them to an audience. But that could take three or four months, and by then the investors would be bankrupt. For the Actors' Equity Association, the closed shop union to which all professional actors must belong, requires that its members be paid full salaries after three or four weeks of rehearsals; all other union members get regular pay from the first. Under this payroll burden, the producer must continue his preparations in cities like ours, selling tickets for seats while he and his associates work frantically to make everything work. Occasionally, to keep the system going, he has already managed to give his new show all but its final flourishes before opening here. He has smoothed off some of the rough edges in a three-day stand at New Haven. His new comedy, let us say, is fresh and funny and needs only a little trimming, or timing. Our people go, are pleased, a little flattered that they have "seen it before New York". In too many cases, however, what we see is patently unfinished.

Boston playgoers are patient, well-disposed to the theater, and many of them are so eager to see the newest hits before they reach Broadway and tickets become unavailable except to those who can afford the black market, that they more or less willingly run all the obvious risks. Others, those who have had too many unpleasant experiences, now stay away from our playhouses altogether, waiting till they can go to New York for a playgoing spree; over there, they know, shows may be bad, too, but they are at least finished.

For the loyal thousands, the eager ones, who continue to try their luck here, there are three major playhouses, two of which, the Colonial and Shubert, present all kinds of legitimate attractions; the third, the Wilbur, is reserved for plays without music, which usually means one-set comedies of contemporary life which are most economical to produce and, when successful, most profitable.

Of these theaters, the **Colonial** is the handsomest. Opened on December 19, 1900, decorated lushly in the rococo style, it has recently been restored to something like its original appearance and although its marquee was modernized and made ugly in the process, the interior was renewed in generally good taste. The lobby is finished in Pompeian marble. From the inner foyer, a stairway leading to the first balcony is remarkable for a bronze bannister. (The second balcony is reached by another stairway on the outside; in 1900, second balcony goers were not permitted to use the same entrance as their better-heeled fellows of the lower levels.) Horace Armistead, who supervised the redecoration of the Colonial in 1960, was not allowed to invest in new damask panels for the walls, but he managed to find substitute materials to carry out the general scheme of warm opulence which was originally built into the Colonial and which gives it, even now, its charm.

From "Ben-Hur", its first tenant, to the latest tryout of our times, the Colonial has played most of the significant productions of the American theater and its comfortable, though not luxurious dressing rooms, have housed all the great stars of the past sixty-five years. Its boxoffice men are generally

The Colonial Theater, interior

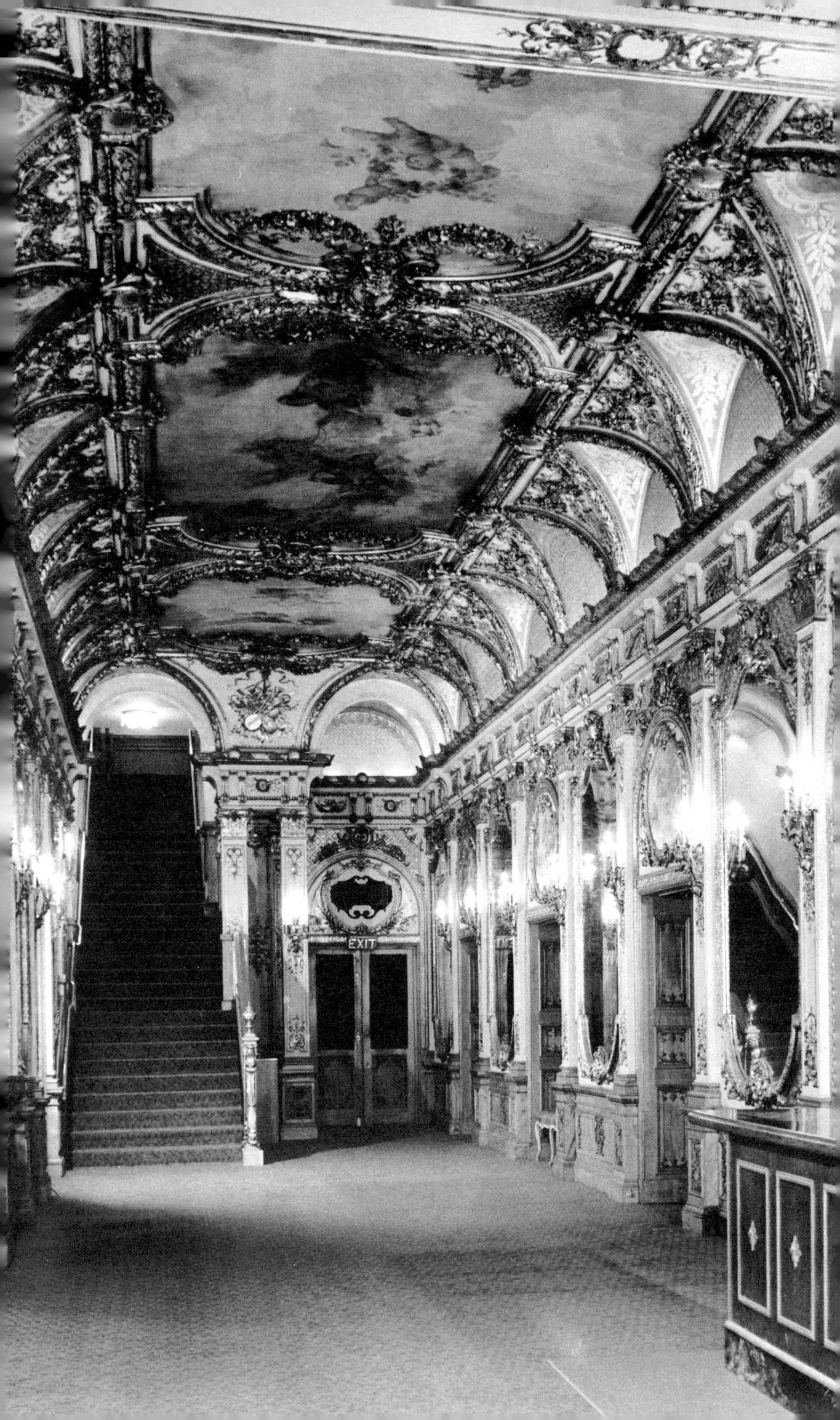
EXIT

courteous, its ushers and attendants gracious, its management efficient. Although it has presented its share of dismal dramas, some half-baked and some which never should have been put into the oven, it still stands for something fine, something admirable. It is located at 100 Boylston Street, in the Colonial Building, opposite Boston Common. Around the corner, two blocks up Tremont street, the **Shubert** is as old as the Colonial to the year, and it too, has a long history of big and little hits and disasters.

For many years, it was the key house of the Boston chain owned or operated by the late Lee and J. J. Shubert. Since 1956, when the Justice Department required the Shuberts to divest themselves of excess properties, it has been their sole playhouse in this city.

In 1956, there were seven legitimate theaters in Boston, and though only three were really active, the others had a few attractions each year; and, in any case, it was good to know they were all there, with their stages ready and their dressing rooms open though dusty. At that time, in addition to the Colonial, the Wilbur and the Shubert, we could also point with some pride (qualified by the faded conditions of one or another) to the Boston Opera House, the Copley, the Majestic and Plymouth theaters. The Shuberts had bought or built all but the Wilbur, which they were operating on a lease when the Justice Department stepped in. While the government was proceeding against them as a "monopoly", these landlords were having problems with the Opera House. Like some other buildings in our Back Bay, which is, of course, made land, it was supported on piles. (This is also true of Symphony Hall, home of the Boston Symphony Orchestra).

The piles needed reinforcement. Rather than pay the estimated cost at $350,000 J. J. Shubert sold it. Today a newly-built dormitory of Northeastern University stands on its site, on Huntington Avenue. Just as abruptly, the Shuberts also sold the Colonial, dropped their lease on the Wilbur, then rented the Plymouth, the Majestic and Copley to a movie exhibitor, who now operates the Majestic as the Saxon and the Plymouth as the Gary, presenting first-run films.

The Copley, built originally and operated for a number of years as a stock and repertory house, was razed last year to make way for the swooping series of ramps which will admit automobilists to a new extention of the Massachusetts Turnpike in Copley Square.

Getting back to the Shubert; it seats 1700 on its orchestra floor, in its two balconies and boxes; it is comfortable, clean, air-conditioned and efficient. It is not and never was handsome.

Diagonally opposite, on Tremont Street, the **Wilbur** is more modern than either the Shubert or the Colonial and rather beautiful, though its beauty has not recently been pointed up. When it was opened in 1914, it was proudly called "the first of the new intimate theaters in Boston". It has 1200 seats. The exterior is faced in dark Harvard brick, with a Colonial balcony over the entrance. The windows of the main doorways are designed after the style of some of the old Beacon Hill homes, with white marble trim. The auditorium is ingeniously constructed to create a sense of intimacy between playgoers and players, who can almost reach out to one another and, when the play is good, sometimes seem to be doing just that.

Boston has other theaters and halls where occasional, or special, attractions of a theatrical kind can play. We also have two off-Broadway theaters of modest proportions.

On Massachusetts Avenue, opposite the rear of the Christian Science Mother Church, an old movie house of vast size and faded splendor, called now the **Back Bay Theater,** accommodates an occasional ballet company and is present headquarters for the Boston Opera, which, under the direction of Sarah Caldwell now presents five operas each year with such stars of eminence as Joan Sutherland.

Farther downtown, the **John Hancock Hall** in the Hancock Insurance Company building, is used by another local organization, the Boston Ballet Company, which, with a new Ford Foundation grant, has just taken on professional size and stature with some artistic help from the New York City Ballet.

Since the demolition of the old Boston Opera House, the Metropolitan Opera Company has been housed, during its annual visit, in a huge movie theater, the **Boston Music Hall,** on Tremont Street, directly across from the Shubert. Although its stage is shallow, the Music Hall has also served the Royal Ballet of England and the Leningrad Kirov Ballet.

On February 21, 1965, the City of Boston provided new facilities for opera and ballet companies. The $12,000,000 **War Memorial Auditorium,** on Boylston Street in the shadow of the new 52-story Prudential Tower, was built primarily for huge meetings of industrial conventioneers. But because the members of the Boston Opera Association raised $361,000 to equip it with a proper stage, dressing rooms and orchestra pit, it will also be used from now on — until we can get something better — as a "Boston Opera House". Its stage is eighty-eight feet wide, forty-two feet deep. Its orchestra pit will accommodate one hundred musicians. On a huge floor, with movable seats, and in a vast horseshoe balcony, it will accommodate 4600 opera goers. This spring, the Metropolitan of New York will present eight operas in this new municipal auditorium, testing its acoustical panels, and the Moiseyev Ballet of Russia will dance on its stage for three successive days. Most of the visiting ballet companies will be accommodated here in the future.

The Auditorium is designed for flexible use rather than for beauty, but it is, in some ways, attractive. The facade over the main entrance of the building is stippled with twenty-two carat gold-faced terra cotta and porcelain enamel on aluminum panels. The foyer is faced with Botticino marble and, in places, with French rouge antique marble. The architects are the Boston firm of Hoyle, Doran and Berry.

Our local off-Broadway theaters are tiny and completely devoid of gold and marble. They are unpretentious. The oldest, the **Charles Playhouse,** occupies what was once a church building, and for a much longer time, a night club, behind the Shubert Theater. It seats 500 on a main floor and a balcony extended on three side of a projecting stage. **The Bostonian PlayHouse** can accommodate at the most ninety-five friendly playgoers, at least a few of whom must be able to see around rather substantial uprights.

The Charles Company, which was started in 1957 by students of Boston University in an upstairs room over a fish market on Charles Street, has progressed from ambitious amateurism to a sketchy professional basis. Some of its productions have been admirable, adventurous and competent; others have been badly acted.

At the Bostonian, on Hemenway Street in the Back Bay, the Theater Company of Boston, Inc., has managed to hold on for three seasons, presenting for the most part dramas of the avant garde. Although performances have sometimes been drearily ineffective, their actors have kept a generally high standard and much of their work has been most interesting.

On another level, some of the colleges of Greater Boston have something to offer to the general playgoer from time to time.

Boston University, for example, presents its student actors of the division of theater arts to the public four times a year in productions directed by faculty members or visiting professionals from New York. Their workshop, the Boston University Theater, on Huntington Avenue opposite Symphony Hall, was built in 1925 largely by public subscription as the Civic Repertory Theater, for producer Henry Jewett. At the time, it was one of the admirable "intimate" playhouses of the country. It would surely become a great home for a great repertory company; or so we believed. But the movies began to talk two years later, and in 1930 it was closed down.

Drama

At **Harvard,** where there is no professional theater program, the students have a magnificent new playhouse which is used almost entirely by them for their own productions. Designed by Hugh Stubbins, opened in 1960, their Loeb Drama Center is two stories high, the exterior of red brick and glass, screened ingeniously in white metal. This "pushbutton playhouse" has a main auditorium seating about 600 and a small bare room that can accommodate one hundred for experimental dramas.

The theater is magnificently equipped with machinery designed by George C. Izenour of Yale. For modern realistic drama, its stage is a roomy proscenium, which seems permanent. At the touch of a button backstage, this can be transformed by a projecting apron. Another button causes seats in the auditorium to swing around to the sides, creating a three-quarters arena.

During the winter, the Harvard Dramatic Club and similar undergraduate groups share this magical pushbutton palace. In July and August, for the six

Loeb Drama Center, Harvard University, rehearsal in the auditorium

weeks duration of the Harvard Summer School, it is opened to the Greater Boston public by the Harvard Summer School Players, a semi-professional company, who offer three or four classic dramas in more or less acceptable performances.

Brandeis University, in nearby Waltham, whose mentors have always been favorable to the theater, is about to open a new $3,500,000 theater facility which will be used primarily by the Theater Arts Department, but will show its share of professional productions to the people of the area in a way that seems, in prospect, exciting.

The Spingold Theater Arts Center, designed by Max Abramowitz, the exterior in brick around a rising central stage tower, will contain not one but three playhouses. The largest of these, seating 700 on the main floor and in one balcony, will have a proscenium stage. The others, of 300 and 100 capacity, will be adjustable to any kind or period of theatrical presentation. Class-

Spingold Theater Arts Center, Brandeis University (architect's rendering)

Drama

rooms and offices of the Theater Art faculty are being built into the structure, which could become a perfect intimate theater workshop. Most stimulating is the Brandeis plan to bring in, at least once a year, a major director, author, or producer with carte blanche to create a full professional production; also, to present resident companies from other parts of the country who have never played Boston. The Brandeis prospects are bright and the plans will benefit not only the University community but also the theatergoers of Boston, who need all the help they can get.

ELLIOT NORTON
Drama Critic
Boston Record American

Legitimate Theaters

Colonial Theater
106 Boylston Street.   426-9366

Shubert Theater
265 Tremont Street.   426-4520

Wilbur Theater
252 Tremont Street.   426-9366

Theaters

Back Bay Theater
209 Massachusetts Avenue.   267-5178

Boston Music Hall
268 Tremont Street.   423-3300

John Hancock Hall
180 Berkeley Street.   421-2000

War Memorial Auditorium
900 Boylston Street.   262-8100

Off-Broadway

Bostonian Playhouse
1138 Boylston Street.   536-2521

Charles Playhouse
76 Warrenton Street.   542-3325

Universities

Boston University Theater
264 Huntington Avenue.   536-9121

Loeb Drama Center
64 Brattle Street, Cambridge.   864-2630

The Spingold Theater Arts Center
Brandeis University
415 South St., Waltham.   894-6000

Boston City Hall, School Street (Central Business District). Architects: Gridley J. Fox Bryant and Arthur Gilman. 1862–65

8 Traditional Architecture

Those manifold and pervasive historic factors which have made Boston distinctive have in turn predisposed the development of an individual school of architecture. One of the most dominant factors has been the topography of the original Boston peninsula, which was extremely irregular in both plan and elevation. Because of Boston's early foundation in 1630, a late medieval, English-derived organic town plan developed around the many hills and coves. The winding, narrow "cow path" streets, the lanes and alleys, the courts and "squares," really left over spaces at irregular street intersections, are still evident throughout the oldest sections of Boston. Virtually no street there originally ran more than three blocks without a change in width, axis, or grade. Thus Boston became the only major city in the country without the standard grid street pattern. In the dense, intimate and pedestrian-scaled plan of Boston, buildings and their walls had to adapt to irregular sites, which gave the town a random appearance. Moreover, there were no large, regular squares or broad, major streets on which to "display" buildings. As a result it was generally not the individual building, but the collective facade that dominated. For example, Boston's great Second Empire **City Hall** is almost lost on its set-back site on a narrow side street. Traditionally the random, lean silhouettes of spires and cupolas announced the presence of meetinghouses or public structures which otherwise nestled in the community of buildings. Equally traditional is that most Boston architecture is directly related to the ground. Thus the great podia and symbolic flights of steps in front of public buildings in other Eastern cities generally do not appear in Boston, as a comparison between the **Boston Public Library** and its New York counterpart indicates.

Topography also influenced the siting of structures because, unlike New York, Philadelphia and Washington where the classic grid plans obliterated many topographic features, Boston was decisively divided into neighborhoods or "compartments" by natural features. Even though the hills were cut down and the coves filled in, to increase the original land area almost four times, Boston's neighborhoods, with such "place" names as the North End, the Colonial South End and the West End (which includes Beacon Hill), remained distinct and developed at different times. Each grew up densely almost to resemble separate small villages. For example, the **Old North Meetinghouse (Second Church)** on North Square in the North End almost paralleled the meetinghouse on the green of a New England village. Boston's resultant compartmentalization clearly demonstrates that it was not conceived as a metropolis as were Philadelphia, Washington and, later in its history, New York.

In addition to the original neighborhoods of Boston Proper and to those on the extensively reclaimed lands, during the nineteenth century Boston absorbed many surrounding towns, such as Charlestown and Roxbury, which had their own architectural traditions, and thus are not considered here.

A second conditioning factor on Boston architecture is dematerialism. The hostile weather and unyielding soil of New England, together with a long tradition of puritan asceticism presupposed the denial of the material. The effect is manifest in Boston architecture in a trend toward the non-plastic and the abstract. Surfaces traditionally are planar and edges crisp; detail is sparse and has limited projection. Materials are few, such as brick, granite and puddingstone; in them superb craftsmanship, rather than bravura techniques, creates the aesthetic effect.

Conservatism has also been a dominant factor of Boston architecture. Thus several selected architectural types persisted, and often "made do" for a variety of functions. For example, the **Old South Meetinghouse** (1729) was seemingly incongruously inspired by an Anglican church ("**Old North**," 1723). Too, many Victorian structures owe evident inspiration to Colonial prototypes. Conservatism is also attributable to puritan Congregationalism. Thus, architecturally all the characteristics of the puritan "Plain Style" are seen in essence in the Boston tradition. Anglican elegance was even tempered, as seen in the relatively austere exteriors of **Christ Church** ("Old North") and the **King's Chapel** (1749–54). Conservatism is also a result of most of the present residential areas of Boston Proper having been built by land developers, whose taste is traditionally standard.

In addition to influences from these factors, Boston architecture has taken its form as the immediate physical expression of the Boston style of living. Whereas style, as an aesthetic entity, has been a major aspect of New York and Philadelphia architecture, Boston has transformed extraneous patterns into something distinctly Bostonian. Even up to the Civil War comparatively few styles are found in Boston, and these are treated so conservatively that one is tempted to call Boston architecture, especially the dominant vernacular domestic modes, "Bostonian." Thus, it is judicious to consider Boston architecture in terms not merely of stylistic development, but also of such factors as topographic and socio-economic development, the historic emergence of individual personalities, like Bulfinch, and historic events, such as the great fires of 1711 and 1872.

Just as Boston's original plan was late medieval English inspired, so too was its early architecture. This is in contrast to more "modern" cities, such as Philadelphia (1683), which essentially began with classical planning and

Traditional Architecture

Bonwit Teller (Originally **Museum of Natural History**), Berkeley and Boylston Streets (Back Bay). Architect: William G. Preston. 1862

The Cultural Resources of Boston

Third Harrison Gray Otis House
(Currently American Meteorological Society), 45 Beacon Street (Beacon Hill). Architect: Charles Bulfinch. 1806

architecture. Most of the seventeenth century buildings were half timber, late medieval yeomen's "cottages," as exemplified by the famous **Paul Revere House** (c. 1677) on North Square. Even the great first Town House (1657), with its strategic central location at the head of State Street (the site of the present **Old State House**), was basically domestic in form except for its open ground floor used as a market and exchange.

A new period in Boston architecture was initiated by such structures as the now demolished "Triangular" warehouse (c. 1680) and the Peter Sargeant House (1679), both significantly in brick and grand in scale and style. These showed — just fifty years after its foundation — Boston's supreme position in the Colonies, which it was to hold until Philadelphia's ascendancy in the mid-eighteenth century. While these were "Jacobean" in style, the magnificent brick **Foster-Hutchinson House** of 1691, formerly near the Paul Revere House, became the first classical structure in New England. This and the Clark-Frankland House, the "Old Brick" Meetinghouse, and the famous second Town House (now known as the **Old State House**), all built of brick after the great fire of 1711, were among the most impressive buildings in all the Colonies. All pre-Georgian in style, they were nonetheless the exception in the townscape. More typical were the brick houses of successful merchants like the extant **Thomas Crease House** (today the **Old Corner Bookstore,** 1712), the **Pierce-Hichborn House** (c. 1710), and the **Clough House** (between 1711 and 1715). Though pre-Georgian, the latter two have the five bay facade and central hall plan which were to become typical in the pre-Revolutionary period. Such merchants' houses were almost always free standing or, at most, in pairs. They were set at the street line either parallel to it or, not infrequently, perpendicular to allow for the necessary urban densities and a certain degree of privacy. Small gardens were set at the side or rear of the house.

The basic elements of the post-1680 period of substantial brick merchants' houses and of several major public structures essentially continued until the Revolution. Densities increased so that the townscape saw even more of the seemingly haphazardly scattered single houses and of public buildings and meetinghouses with their lean silhouettes. While some of the public structures, especially those that represented the Crown, were elegant monuments, they were now hardly as resplendent as those in Philadelphia. Notable pre-Revolutionary structures include **Christ Church ("Old North"** of 1723), the **Old South Meetinghouse** (1729) and **Faneuil Hall** (1740–42). The Hall shows that about 1735–40 the academic forms of neo-Palladianism began to appear in Boston; it remains among the earliest public examples of this new mode in the City. The crowning architectural achievement of this period is the sumptuous interior of **King's Chapel** (1749-55), significantly an Anglican church and designed by the worldly Peter Harrison of Newport. Generally, however, the neo-Palladian or "Georgian" (a convenient, but usually meaningless term because of its overly broad application) resulted in adjustments in scale and proportion, made gable ends have lower pitches to resemble classical pediments and supplied a new vocabulary of details. This is of historic interest; yet, since the basic forms, especially of the vernacular domestic architecture, evolved slowly, it would be academic to define a distinctive Georgian phase.

The post-Revolutionary architecture of Boston centered around the personality of Bulfinch and, to a large extent, Beacon Hill which he originally planned, adorned with great mansions, and crowned with the new **State House** (1795-98). The urbanity, monumentality, elegance and originality of Bulfinch's designs were revolutionary. He introduced a variety of specific new types including his five churches, theater, hospitals, public and residential structures, *inter alia*. Also notable are his town plans, which introduced the crescent as an orderly and monumental focus for residences, and his various developments which included a waterfront plan centering around the **India Wharf**. Though sections of the City are seventeenth century in plan, most of the architecture and plan of Boston is nineteenth century and traces many of its forms, directly or indirectly, to Bulfinch. For the "restrained elegance" of Bulfinch was to be the perfect form through which the *modus vivendi* of Boston expressed itself for most of the following century.

Critical appraisal demonstrates that Bulfinch was one of the most consistently tasteful and prolific architects of the Federal period. While he did introduce the Federal (Adamesque) style to New England, significantly upon his return from a trip to England, the Federal style made its first appearance in the country in Philadelphia with such *cognoscenti* as William Hamilton and John Penn. Moreover, while several of Bulfinch's designs are nationally significant, the majority of his *oeuvre* is traditionally Bostonian and easily takes its place in the total cityscape. For this, among other reasons, Bulfinch was not as significant as his contemporaries, Jefferson and Latrobe. Likewise he was not as influential; while his manner inspired McIntyre, Damon and Benjamin, it was the publications of the last which spread the Federal style. Perhaps Bulfinch's approach is best summarized in his design of the first **Harrison Gray Otis House**. While Bulfinch described the Bingham Man-

West Church, 131 Cambridge Street (West End). Architect: Asher Benjamin. 1806

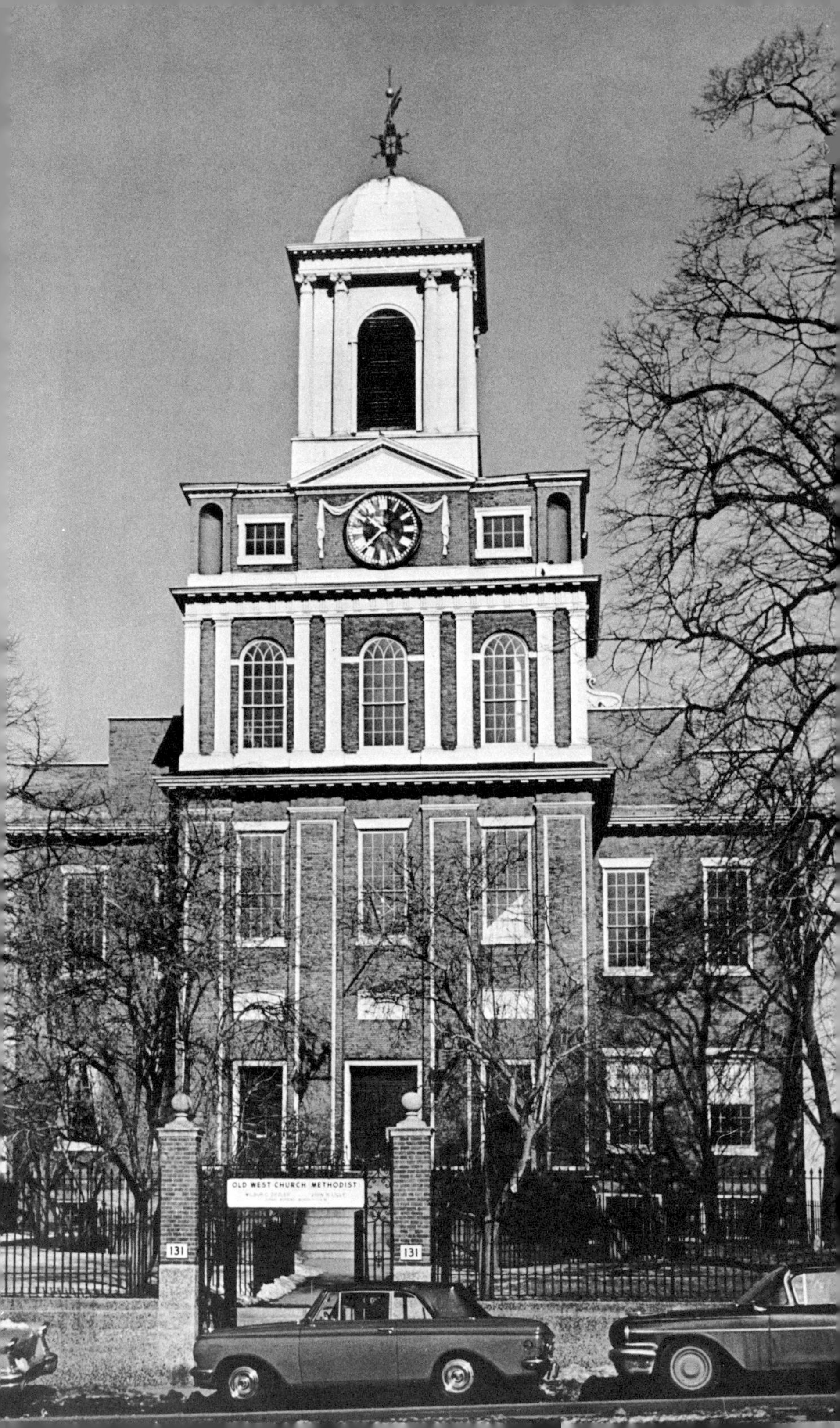
OLD WEST CHURCH METHODIST
131
131

sion in Philadelphia, which he saw in 1789, as being too lavish for any American, he nonetheless took it as his inspiration for the Otis House, which he then made more chaste and smaller in scale.

One of the elements conspicuously lacking in Bulfinch's *oeuvre* is French influence due both to traditional Boston Anglophilia and to President Adams' Federalism. Conversely French influence was an important factor in the Federal architecture of Jefferson and in New York, Philadelphia, and Washington, in all of which L'Enfant left his imprint. Indeed, diaries note that it was almost *de rigueur* to speak French in the "Federal Court" which reigned in the capital of Philadelphia in the 1790's. Paradoxically, while French taste had limited appeal in pre-Victorian Boston, the infatuation with it after mid-century produced historically significant landmarks such as the **Deacon House** (1848), the **City Hall** (Bryant and Gilman, 1862–65), the first major public Second Empire building in the country, and the proto-"City Beautiful" plan of the Back Bay.

In domestic architecture from the Federal to the Civil War periods the forms of Bulfinch and his followers became traditional and received just slight "Victorianizing" modifications in proportions and details. Exotic styles such as the Gothic, Egyptian and Moorish found sporadic representations, mostly in country villa architecture. Interestingly, the row house — most often the row town house — became the dominant form at this time. Yet, this form is not traditional with Boston, as it is with Philadelphia from the late seventeenth century. Indeed Beacon Hill and the South End, today so dense with row houses that the streets seem like open corridors, were originally planned for single houses, mansions or villas.

The Greek Revival in Boston public architecture at first seems weak and insignificant. It produced few major monuments such as those of Philadelphia, the birth- and deathplace of the style in this country. While **St. Paul's Cathedral** (1819–20, Alexander Parris), **Quincy Market** (1824–26, Parris), the demolished **Merchants Exchange** (1842, Isaiah Rogers), and the **Custom House** (1837–47, Ammi B. Young) were among the most important public buildings, none strove for archaeological correctness; indeed St. Paul's should technically not be called Greek Revival, though it was the first example of the temple mode in Boston. Rather, the Greek Revival showed its rational, utilitarian aspect which was thoroughly transformed into an integral part of the Boston school, and the result, which is of highest significance, gives insight to the Boston manner. It is the granite vernacular commercial structures, mainly the waterfront warehouses — such a direct manifestation

Traditional Architecture

of Boston's traditional relation to the sea — that are "hardly equalled anywhere in the world" according to Professor Hitchcock. These combine traditional Boston utility with a natural treatment of granite and with the logicality of engineering principles. For the architects of the Boston granite school were also engineers or vitally interested in engineering, thus resolving the nineteenth century schism between designer and constructor: Parris, Willard, Rogers, Young, Baldwin, Bryant. Granite made its first extensive appearance with Bulfinch, but only became greatly available with the new quarrying and transporting techniques developed for the construction of the **Bunker Hill Monument,** begun in 1825. As a result of the fascination of engineering and of the megalomania inherent in the Greek Revival, granite was less laid in ashlar blocks than used in great, story-high slabs either as post and lintel or, as in the **Pond Building** (34 Merchants Row), as wall surface. The trabeated use is more important for it reveals structure, destroys the traditional concept of a wall skin and opens the building to maximum light and air, employs a sort of prefabricated, and religiously respects the nature of the hard granite which is rarely decorated or treated with non-inherent techniques. **The Sears Block,** at Court Street and Cornhill, rates as one of the most significant structures of its kind. The facade is composed of thinnest possible granite posts and lintels; all else is window! Not only was this more progressive than most cast-iron buildings, the succeeding technology, but it is indeed a prototype of both the skyscraper aesthetic and construction.

Coincident with the Greek Revival granite school is an analogous school of early Gothic Revival granite churches. Approximately two dozen of the churches were built between the mid-eighteen twenties and mid-century. Less than half a dozen remain and these are scattered throughout the entire City; **St. John the Evangelist** at 35 Bowdoin Street (c. 1825, attributed to Willard) is the most accessible, if not the most impressive example. These churches also used granite in large blocks, but rarely in slabs. Though detailing is sparse, it is invariably bold since the merlons, quatrefoil windows or pointed arches are often made from one block. The similarity between the Gothic and Greek Revivals in Boston not only attests to the strength of the Boston school but shows that both are just aspects of the general trend of romanticism, as much as it could assert itself in the conservatism of the area.

The historic year of 1872 marked a hiatus in the Boston school of architecture, which was to last about two decades before the indigenous traditions reasserted themselves. The catastrophic fire of that year in downtown

Boston cleared a large area which was rebuilt in the fashionable styles of the *parvenu* post-Civil War era, which gave Boston the stamp of New York. The Second Empire and High Victorian Gothic insurance, financial and public buildings, many of which still survive in the central business district, gave Bostonians a physical manifestation of their commercial success as did the scale and stylishness of their new houses being built in the Back Bay at this same time. The residences of this area, which had the first executed pure grid plan in Boston Proper, date mainly from 1860 to 1900 and are roughly divided into three phases: Second Empire, Victorian Gothic and Queen Anne, academic revivals. The fire of 1872 had marked the death knoll of the downtown as a residential area and forced the churches there to move; many relocated in the new Back Bay, to which they imparted the same monumentality and assurance found in the newly rebuilt commercial downtown. The Back Bay itself has remained the most complete statement of later Victorian domestic architecture in the country; the quality of both individual houses and of the collective facades makes the area without parallel.

The crucial year of 1872 also found H. H. Richardson designing **Trinity Church** in Copley Square, and thus the commencing of another golden age after Bulfinch and after the granite school. Though trained in this country and abroad, Richardson was a logical continuation of the Boston school. His treatment of materials was natural and honest, and was derived from the earlier granite school; his understanding of function and his concern for clarity created integrated form which reacted to the often capricious, picturesque massing of Victorian Gothic; his treatment of the planarity of wall surfaces, so essentially of the Boston school, clarified the mannered and often confusing richness of later Victorian surfaces. Trinity Church remains one of the masterpieces of American architecture. Its influence and that of Richardson were appreciated, but more often they were misunderstood, as exemplified by the several office buildings in the country which copied Trinty. Though Richardson had many followers in Boston, virtually none had the taste, sureity of hand or inventiveness of the master. His influence is often seen in the "cleaning up" of many of the later Victorian commercial buildings. Yet when Richardson's literal manner was used, it merely degenerated into a convenient decorative vocabulary, even in the hands of his direct *protégés* or, at worst, a superficial mode in which the considerable amount of speculative building at this period cast itself.

The last decades of the nineteenth century saw various classical revivals and the Beaux-arts interpretations. Of the former most important are the Georgian and Federal Revivals. Yet, it is not truly accurate to speak of such

Trinity Church, Copley Square (Back Bay). Architect: Henry Hobson Richardson. 1872–77 (Portico and front towers added 1892)

revivals in Boston for Georgian, Federal and even Greek Revival facade arrangements, forms and details appeared consistently and appreciably throughout the nineteenth century. The situation is analogous to the fact that the classical spirit never really died in Italy, so that the term "renaissance" is not wholly descriptive.

The Beaux-arts styles of the turn of the century are sparsely and often not convincingly represented in Boston. In domestic architecture there are few examples of "Fifth Avenue French *château*" or "Fifth Avenue Italian *palazzo.*" While most of the downtown commercial buildings of this period were cast in the Beaux-arts mold, the forms and details were almost completely transformed into the Boston school. Thus the Boston Beaux-arts often seems timid or weak, especially in comparison to the high fashion Beaux-arts of New York. This is best seen in the *oeuvre* of Shepley, Rutan and Coolidge; though the direct successors of Richardson, they practiced extensively in the Beaux-arts styles. Though their **Boston Safe Deposit and Trust Company** (1908-11) is Roman Eclectic, the extensively planar wall surfaces, the restrained scale, the sparsity and thinness of detail and the relative lack of plasticity unmistakably place it in the Boston school. Because of this, the Trust Company and many other pre-World War I Boston buildings seem to be akin to post-War neo-classicism. A similarly instructive instance can be seen in McKim, Mead and White's **Boston Public Library** (1888-95), that masterpiece which took its form out of respect to Trinity and because it completed Copley Square. Though Renaissance Eclectic in style, the Library is of the Boston school, which is immediately evident in comparison with the Beaux-arts New York Public Library by the firm's *confrère*, Carrere and Hastings. That virtually all McKim, Mead and White's Boston buildings differ from their New York work attests to the sensitivity of the firm and to their early training in Boston and elsewhere in New England.

The architecture of Boston Proper, especially the domestic, may be said to have fully evolved by the turn of the century, or at least by World War I. For by then the effect of the suburban railroad and the automobile was fully evident. For example, the projected development of the Back Bay never materialized. Between the World Wars one finds several dry and academic Federal Revival apartment houses, and several banks, insurance companies, federal buildings, and skyscrapers. The Boston school had spent itself after having given significant form to Boston for three centuries.

J. DANIEL SELIG
Architectural Historian
Boston Redevelopment Authority

Traditional Architecture

Selected Historic House Museums in Boston Proper

Paul Revere House (17th Century)
19 North Sq., North End
Open 10-4 daily except Sunday and Holidays

Pierce-Hichborn House (Pre-Georgian)
29 North Sq., North End
Open November through April: 10-4 weekdays, 2-4 Sundays, closed Tuesday and Holidays; May through October: Harrison Gray Otis House and 10-4 daily except Monday

S.P.N.E.A. Museum (Federal)
141 Cambridge St., West End
Open 10-4 daily except Saturday and Holidays

Rose Standish Nichols House (Federal)
55 Mt. Vernon St., Beacon Hill
Open 2-5 Wednesday and Saturday

Gibson House (Victorian)
137 Beacon St., Back Bay
Open 2-5 daily except Monday and Holidays

Selected Historic Houses in The Outer Neighborhoods

Loring-Greenough House (Georgian)
12 South St., Jamaica Plain

Shirley-Eustis House (Georgian with Federal additions)
Shirley Place, Roxbury

Dillaway-Thomas House (Georgian)
183 Roxbury St., John Eliot Sq., Roxbury

Blake House (17th Century)
Edward Everett Sq., Dorchester

Clapp House (Federal)
195 Boston St., Dorchester

Several of these structures are headquarters for clubs and historical societies. Because of their relative inaccessibility and sporadic visiting hours, they would be of interest mainly to the architectural student.

Selected Historic Structures Adapted to Current Uses

34 Beacon Street (Late Federal)
Little, Brown and Company
39-40 Beacon Street (Late Federal)
Women's City Club of Boston
42 Beacon Street (Classical Revival)
Somerset Club
45 Beacon Street (Federal)
American Meteorological Society
55 Beacon Street (Federal)
Colonial Dames of America
87 Mt. Vernon Street (Federal)
Colonial Society of Massachusetts
41 Union Street (Pre-Georgian)
Union Oyster House
School and Washington Sts. (Pre-Georgian)
Boston Globe ("Old Corner Bookstore")

While some of the above are open to the public during business hours or during special visiting hours, all usually receive visitors by application.

Seeing Boston Architecture

The view from the observation deck of the Custom House Tower shows Boston's organic plan, distinctive neighborhoods, land-filled areas as well as Boston's situation in general: the harbor, surrounding towns, the distant highlands.
While the Georgian and Federal monuments of Boston are deservedly famous, the visitor will find important architecture in the area east of Faneuil Hall, the central business district, South End and Back Bay. More extensive excursions into the outer neighborhoods, especially Charlestown, Roxbury, Jamaica Plain and Dorchester will prove gratifying.

9 Contemporary Architecture

Boston is one of a number of cities in the United States actively involved in rebuilding its central business district and re-housing those who live in the core area. As in Philadelphia and New York, San Francisco, Cleveland, Fort Worth, etc., large amounts of government and private funds are being expended in an attempt to make the city commercially viable and habitable. In the renovation process, prime importance has been and must continue to be given to low income housing. But this alone is not enough. The flight to the suburbs of those of moderate economic potential has left the center city to the economically deprived. A few generations ago they were the immigrant working class but today are the Negro and the Puerto Rican. The result is a more stringent segregation than we have ever known before. New housing built in the core must create a desirable environment for the middle and upper income group as well as satisfactory low cost housing. Boston and Philadelphia have taken a lead in this regard, hoping to encourage a typical cross-section and economic mix in the central city to counter the pernicious influence of the economically segregated suburbs. Marksdale Gardens, Academy Homes, 330 Beacon Street, and Charlesbank Apartments are examples of the diversified housing program currently underway in Boston.

Second only in importance to new housing is the renovation of the central commercial area itself. The variety of shopping and service facilities and places for the transaction of business that exist in a concentrated urban environment benefit commercial and financial interests. In Boston, amidst such undistinguished new architectural achievements as the Prudential Center, the War Memorial Auditorium, and the State Office Building, there are notable additions that serve as splendid examples such as the new State Street Bank, the new State Mental Health Clinic and the State Service Center, the Blue Cross — Blue Shield Building and, above all, the new Boston City Hall.

Third in importance to any Metropolitan district are those buildings dedicated to education — grade schools, high schools, private schools, colleges, and universities. In urban areas schools and colleges educate those who will work in and administer the cities of the future. At the same time, in contrast to the green-grass schools, they may by example provide both an idea and a long and fruitful exposure to what urban life may be. The building programs of the major universities in the Boston area have, both financially and aesthetically, decisively influenced the development of the city. New buildings at Boston University, Harvard, and M.I.T. are notable in this regard while, at the same time, their administrations have been particularly sensitive to the financial and transportation problems they engender in the community.

Contemporary Architecture

The buildings in this small group have been selected because they rise above mere provision of adequate volumes for desultory human activity. They seek to solve some of the major issues of our day. In solving them they hope to provide in addition to adequate and convenient functioning spaces, environments that are socially, visually and aesthetically stimulating.

> HENRY A. MILLON
> Associate Professor
> of the History of Architecture
> Massachusetts Institute of Technology

Boston University Law and Education Building

From either side of the river the base of this tower is always apparent, disclosing its relationship to the ground terraces and adjacent buildings. Within the tower there is a similar clear differentiation of use spaces as they declare themselves stridently on the exterior. Lecture rooms, classrooms, offices, and cubicles disclose their nature in the variety of surfaces shown on the exterior of the tower. Even the stack from the Boiler Room is brought to the outside and allowed to run the full height of the building, serving thereby, through its dominant continuous verticality as a foil to the horizontal volumetric character of the rooms themselves.

Boston University Law and Education Building. Architect: Sert, Jackson, and Gourley, in association with Edwin T. Steffian (1963).
765 Commonwealth Ave., Boston.

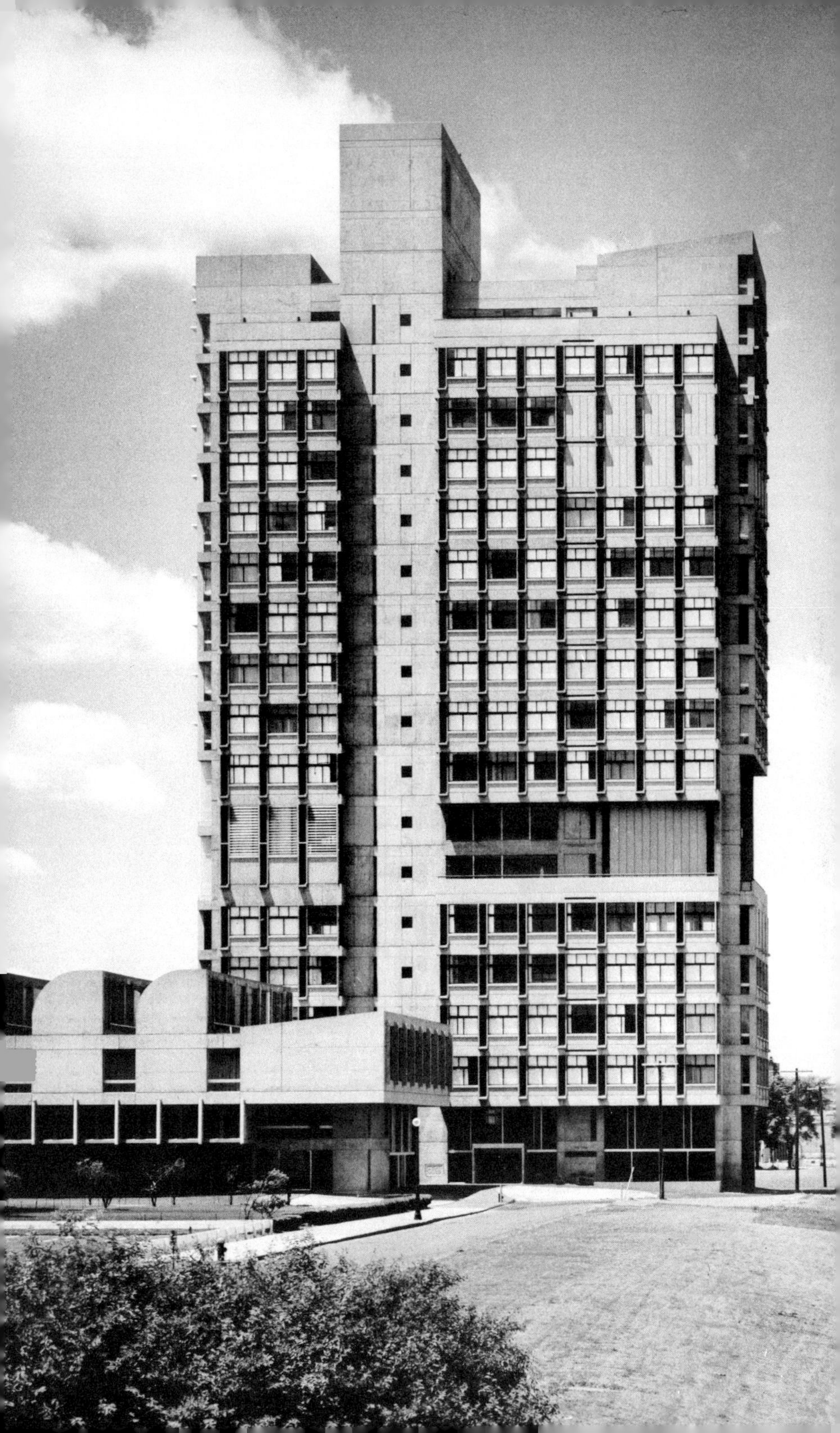

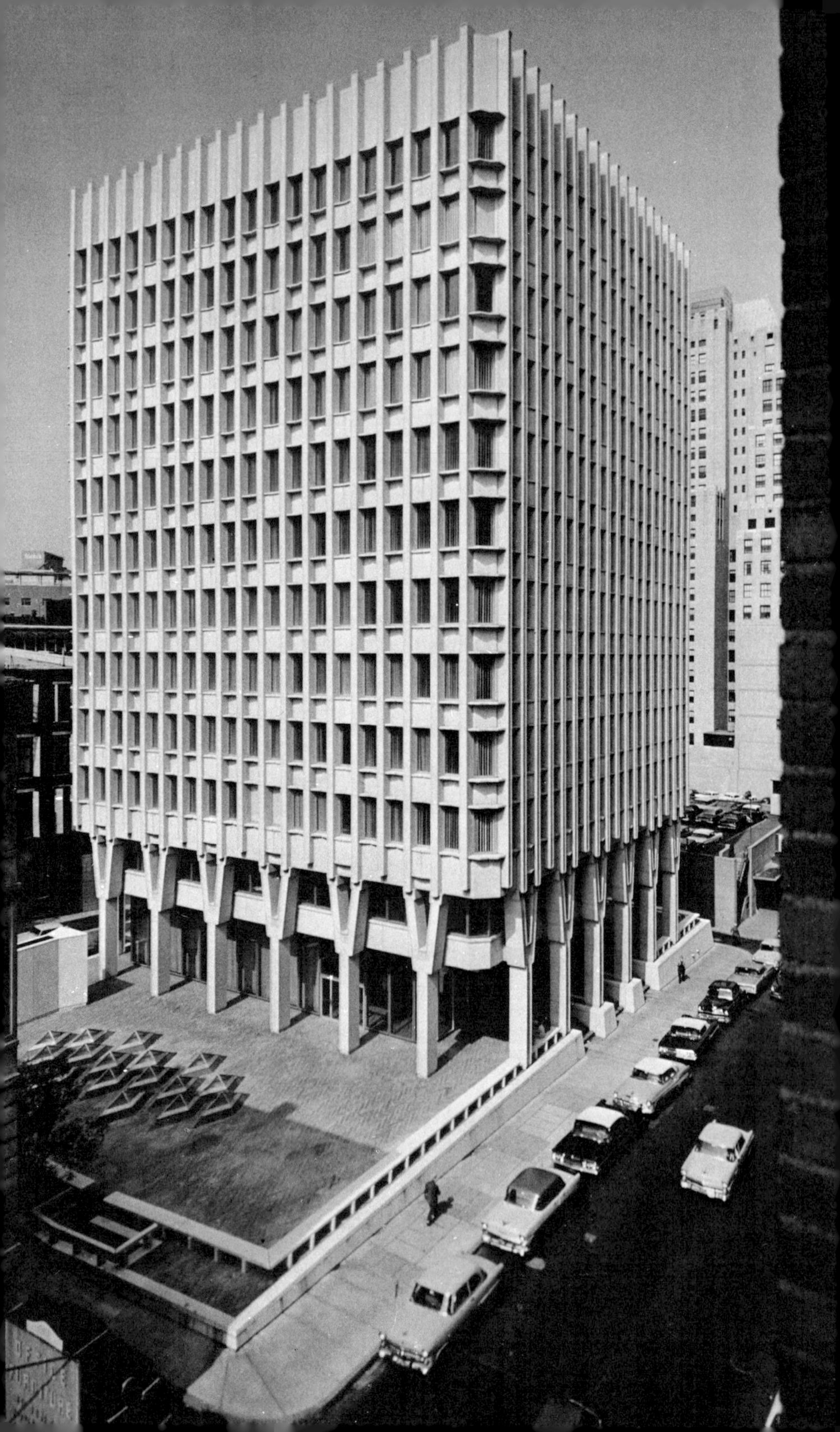

Blue Cross — Blue Shield

The home offices for Blue Cross — Blue Shield are contained in this tower resting on a platform containing mechanical services and cafeteria. The strongly articulated structural system that doubles the number of columns above the main entrance level also includes return and supply air conditioning ducts leading to each of the floors. The architects hoped thereby to make the necessary part of the contemporary office buildings a more expressive part of the building. Particularly noteworthy is the way, on top of the cafeteria to the South, the architects were able to develop the site with benches and potted trees and plants as an amenity for the employees, visitors and public at large.

Blue Cross — Blue Shield Building.
Architect: Paul Rudolph in association with Anderson, Beckwith and Haible (1960).
133 Federal St., Boston.

Charlesbank Apartments

The Charlesbank Apartments, Boston's best high-rise middle income housing, utilizes an economical pre-cast exterior wall construction and an unusual structural system that should allow considerable freedom of unit planning. The plans unfortunately do not, however, realize the full potential of the system for differentiation in response to orientation, view, sunlight, etc. The commanding position of the block on a rise of ground overlooking Huntington Avenue (a major traffic artery) makes the building a prime visual landmark between Boston and Roxbury.

Charlesbank Apartments.
Architect: Hugh Stubbins and Associates, Inc. (1960's).
650 Huntington Ave., Roxbury.

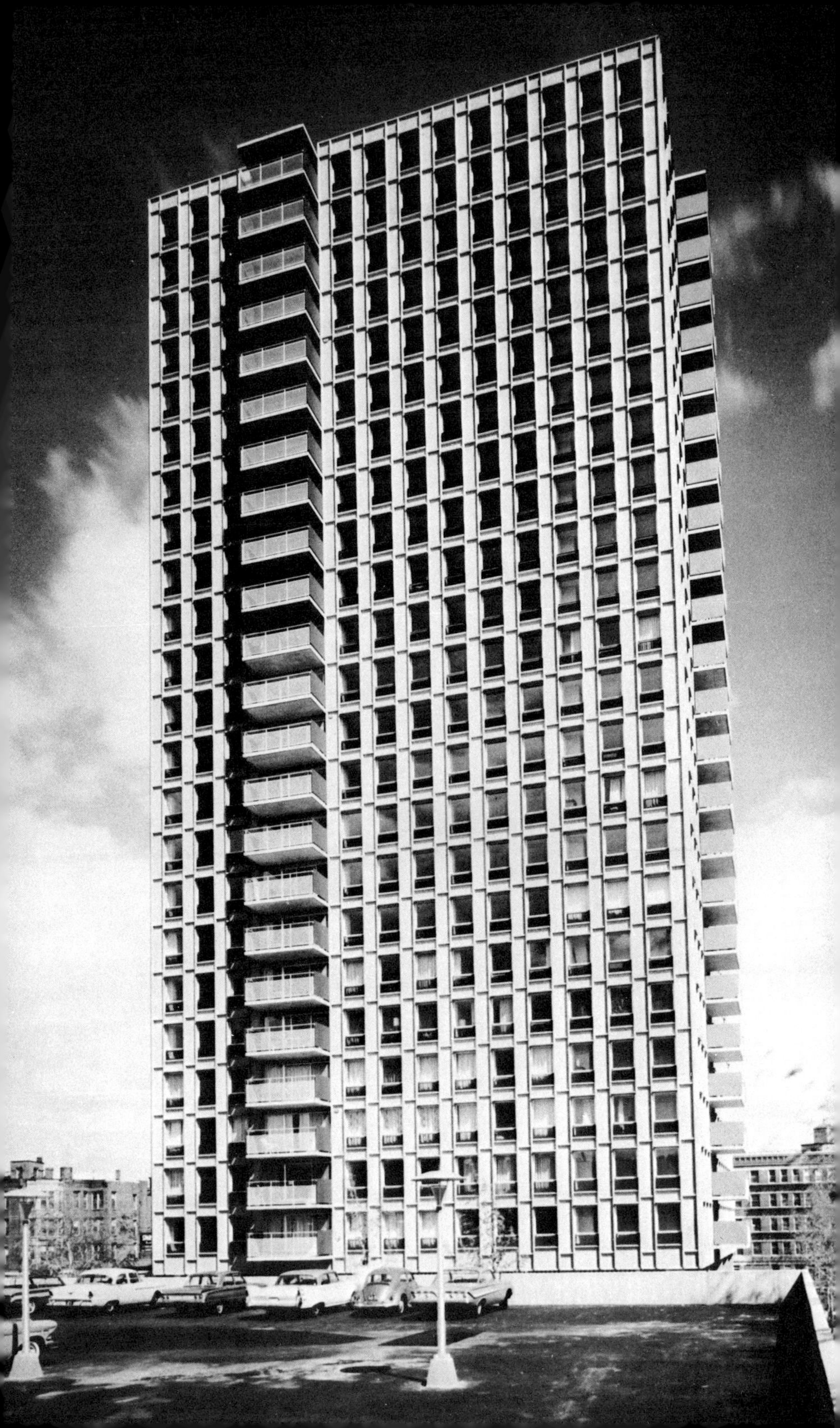

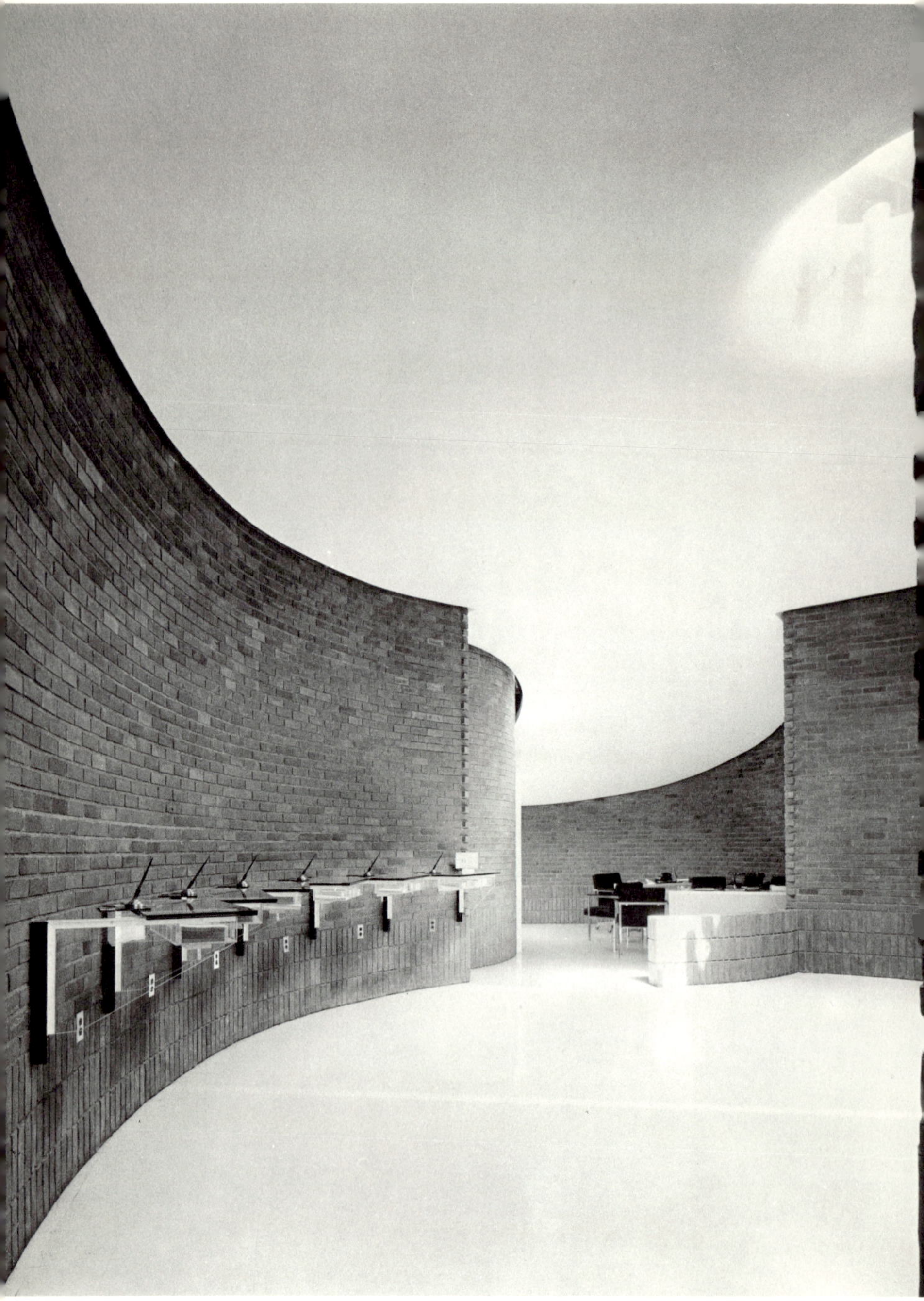

Contemporary Architecture

Shawmut Branch Bank

The Bowdoin Square branch of the National Shawmut Bank is a three-dimensional free-standing sculptural form acknowledging only the access points to the site. It is a delightful spatial toy. A spiral brick wall opens out most invitingly at the entrance where the roof plane, held tautly between the arms of the spiral, sweeps down to the entrance. The interior space rises sharply to a brightly lighted conical central area. The subsidiary brick forms seen from the exterior contain the tellers' spaces and conference rooms. Of particular interest is the varied lighting on these several spaces.

National Shawmut Branch Bank.
Architect: Imre and Anthony Halasz.
Associated architects: Marvin E. Goody
and John M. Clancy, Inc. (1963).
109 Cambridge St., Boston.

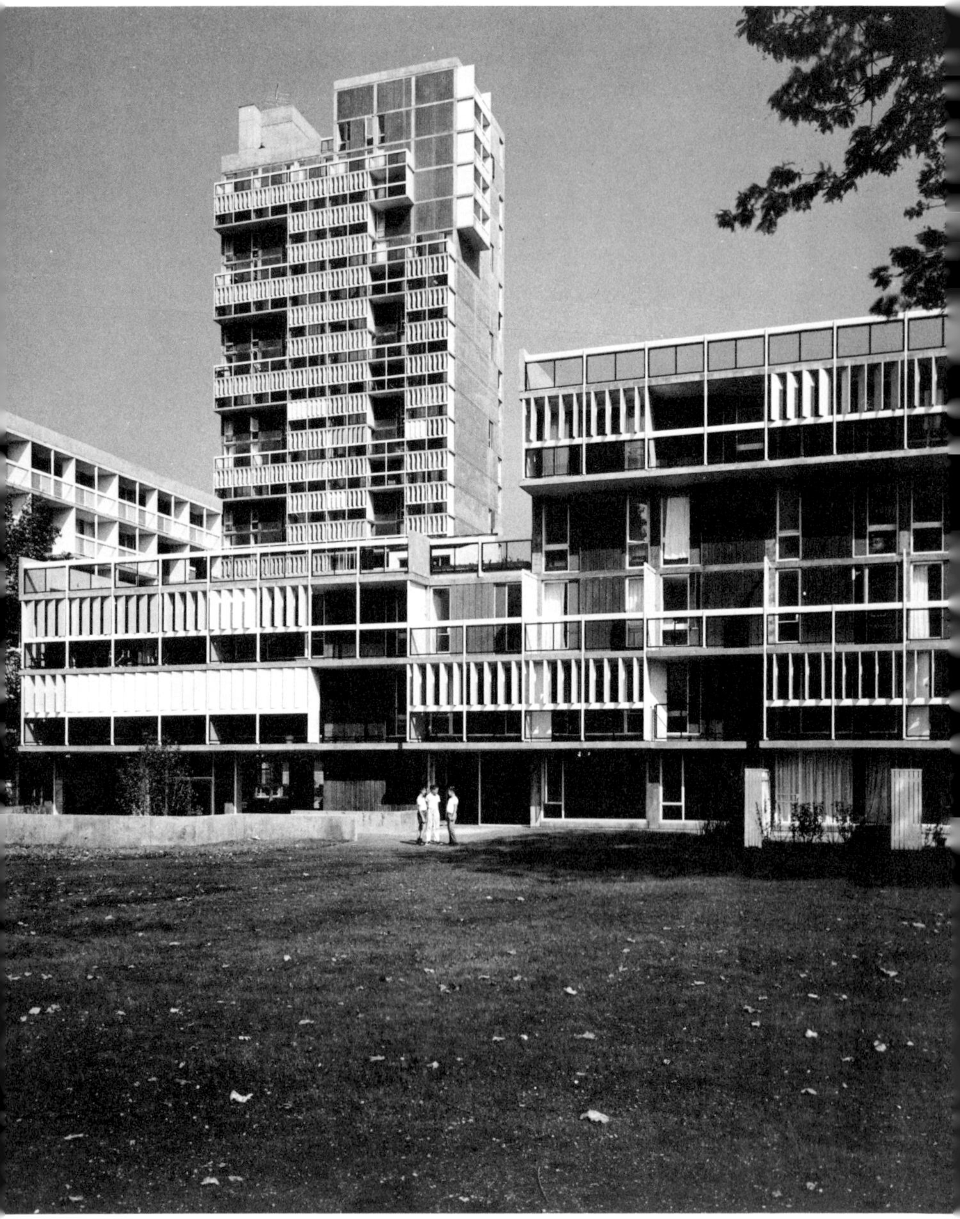

Peabody Terrace

The complex of buildings at Peabody Terrace, Harvard University, speaks most eloquently for an integration of buildings with their surroundings; for intimate and formal exterior use spaces; for a differentiation of units that maximize individuality; for a varied site organization that allows further building to form a continuity with it; and for the individual human needs of sunlight, view, and variety in an urban setting.

Harvard University, Married Students Housing, Peabody Terrace. Architect: Sert, Jackson, and Gourley (1964). Memorial Drive, Cambridge.

Academy Homes

Academy Homes, Marksdale Gardens and other portions of the Washington Park redevelopment area indicate several of the directions pursued in low cost walk-up row housing in Metropolitan Boston. Academy Homes is particularly noteworthy for the contemporary industrial techniques employed in the pre-cast concrete structure (wall, floor, and roof panels, and the exterior metal wall panels) that make up the units. The duplex units with through ventilation unfortunately do not realize the potential flexibility of plan and differentiation of units that such a structural system implies.

Academy Homes. Architect:
Hugh Stubbins and Associates, Inc.
(1963).
Washington Park, Roxbury.

Contemporary Architecture

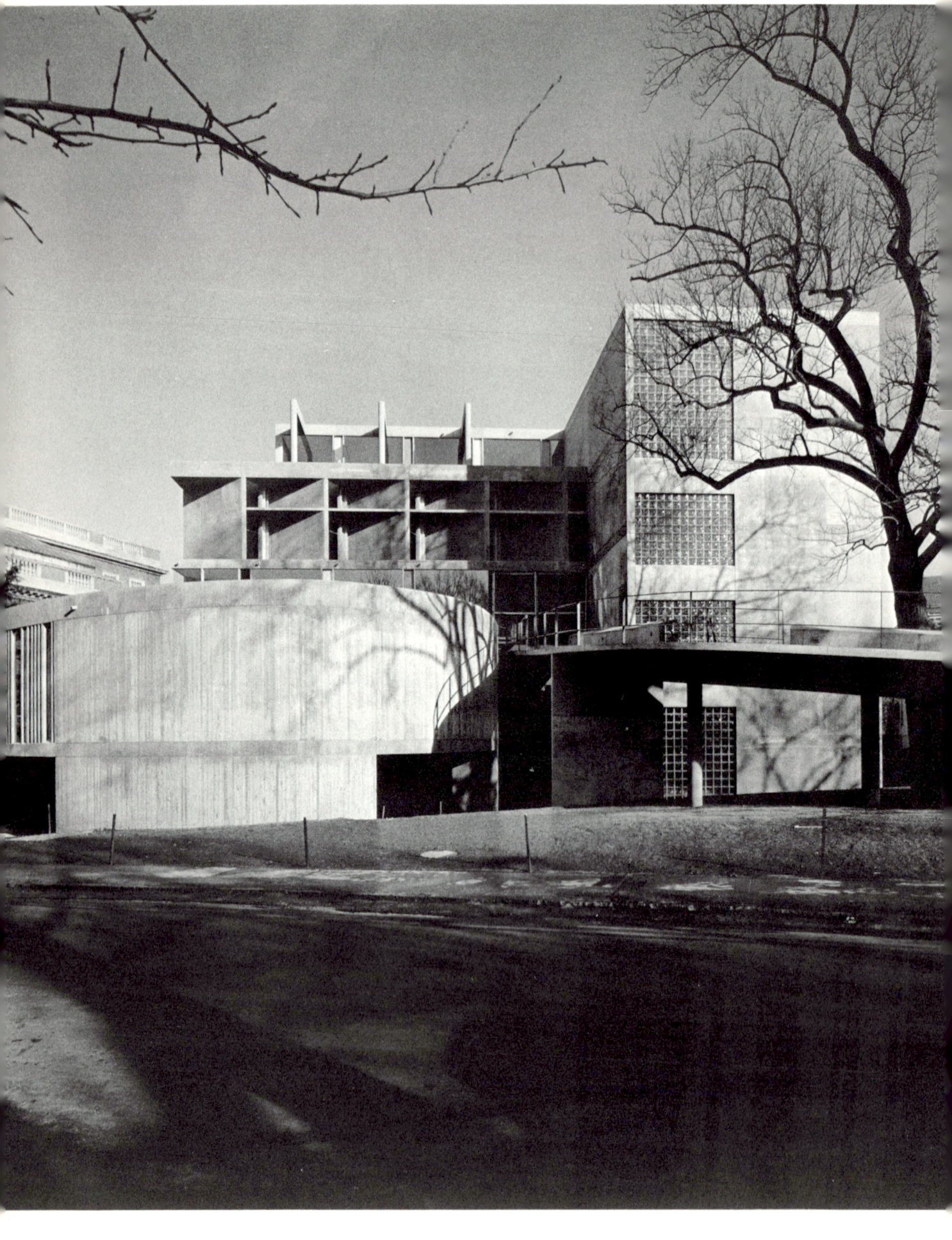

Carpenter Center

Carpenter Center is the only building in the country by the world famed Swiss architect, Le Corbusier and shows well his exceptionally fine handling of a difficult and constricted site. The approaches to the building from the streets on either side show his remarkable ability to integrate the building with its surroundings. The terrace to the rear unites the Fogg Museum and Carpenter Center, displaying to advantage both buildings while it forms a delightful urban space. From the terrace and from Quincy Street, up the ramps and through the building, space flows and weaves itself uninterruptedly, exposing and disclosing the activity spaces within.

Harvard University, Carpenter Center
for the Visual Arts. Architect:
Le Corbusier. Collaborating architects:
Sert, Jackson and Gourley (1962).
19 Prescott St., Cambridge.

Earth Sciences Building, M.I.T.

This prismatic structure contains classrooms, lecture hall, offices, and laboratories. It is a notable addition to, and conscious continuation of, the neoclassical architectural tradition at M.I.T. It is at the same time, however, one of the first tall reinforced concrete buildings and represented for the architect and M.I.T. an experimentation with new construction techniques. This austere and severe structure has become a visual landmark for M.I.T.

M.I.T. Earth Sciences Center. Architect:
I. M. Pei & Associates, Architects (1964).
M.I.T. Campus.

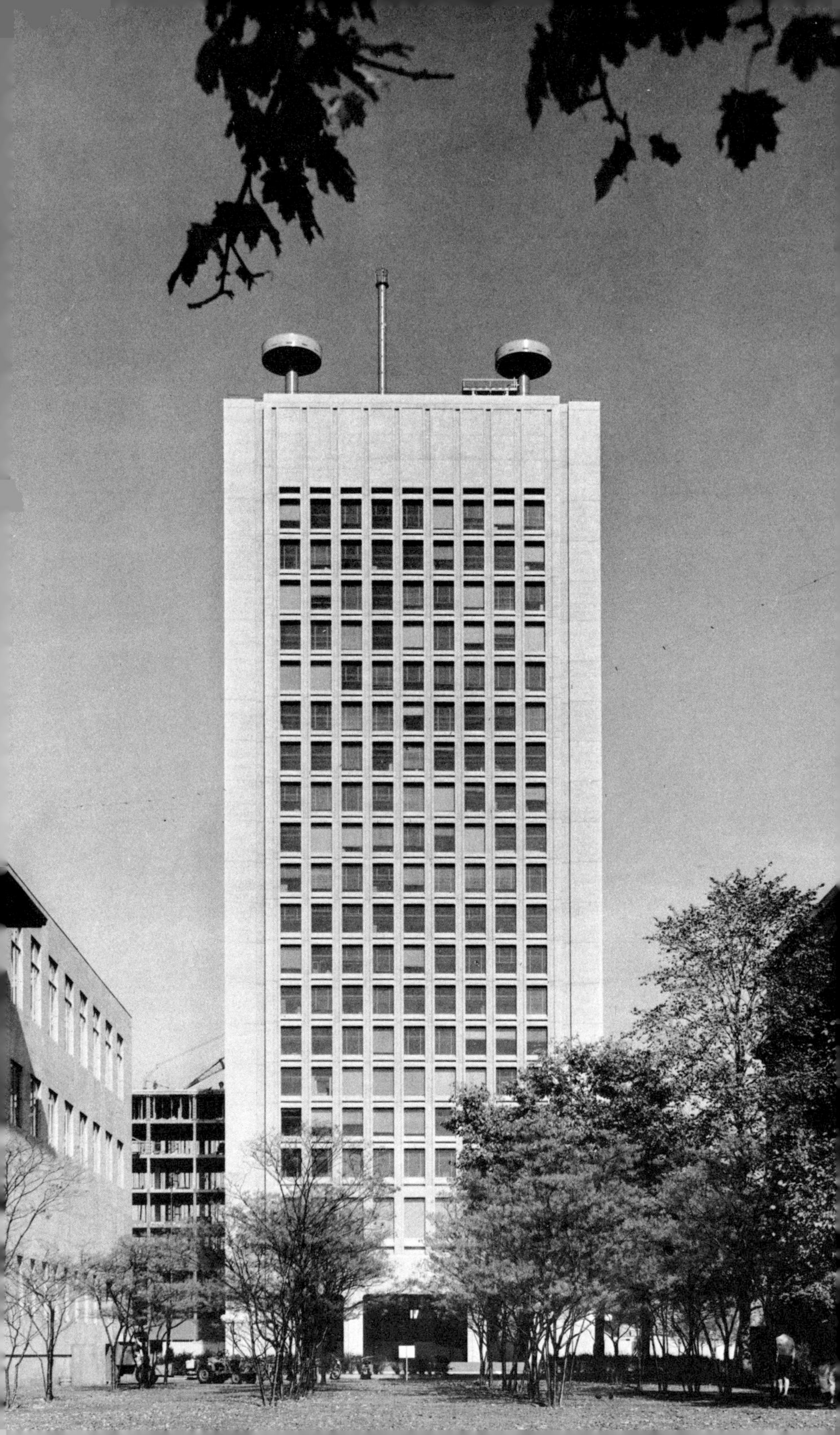

The Cultural Resources of Boston

WGBH's new studio building at 125 Western Avenue was made possible by the contributions of more than 50,000 persons and organizations after the station's old quarters were burned in 1961. The building contains the largest television studio in New England and broadcasting equipment surpassed only by the major networks.

10 Educational Television

About a year ago, the Sunday Globe published a special supplement called "Boston: City of Culture." The supplement devoted a full page to educational television and radio station WGBH, and in it Globe writer Robert Levey aptly described the role that the station plays in this city's culture. For nearly a decade, Levey wrote, WGBH-TV, Channel 2 "has been frankly and fondly bridging the gap between the city's people and its famed academic and artistic centers. Since the station began to broadcast on May 2, 1955, Boston residents have gradually come to know that there is nothing gray and tepid about the traditional institutions of the city; rather there is freshness and excitement, beauty and knowledge, the unique and the enriching. Harvard, M.I.T., Boston Symphony, the Museum of Fine Arts — things familiar in name to any Bostonian — have long brought world recognition to this city, but to many of those who live here they were just locations. Channel 2 has worked constantly to bring alive Boston's bastions of learning and culture for the benefit of anyone who wished to turn on his television set. It is, of course, life that was always there, but was hidden from much of the population."

We live at a time when our universities and our cultural institutions are moving into the mainstream of American life. The old distinction between town and gown is rapidly disappearing. So, one would hope, is the anti-intellectualism that has been so prominent in American history. Our intellectual centers are contributing to every phase of our society and it is clear that these institutions are among our most important engines of progress. More and more it is vital for every man to know what is happening behind the walls of our universities and our cultural institutions.

And this, as Mr. Levey points out, is a chief reason why WGBH is significant in the Boston community. It is a link between the ordinary citizen and the world of the intellect and culture that lies so close by yet so far away.

More than to any one thing, WGBH owes its success and its place in Boston to its close association with the 13 institutions that are members of the Lowell Institute Cooperative Broadcasting Council. These institutions make available to WGBH their vast reservoirs of skill and talent. But they also, and this is too little understood, supply each year a significant part of the station's regular operating budget.

Here is the full list so that the reader may appreciate its weight:

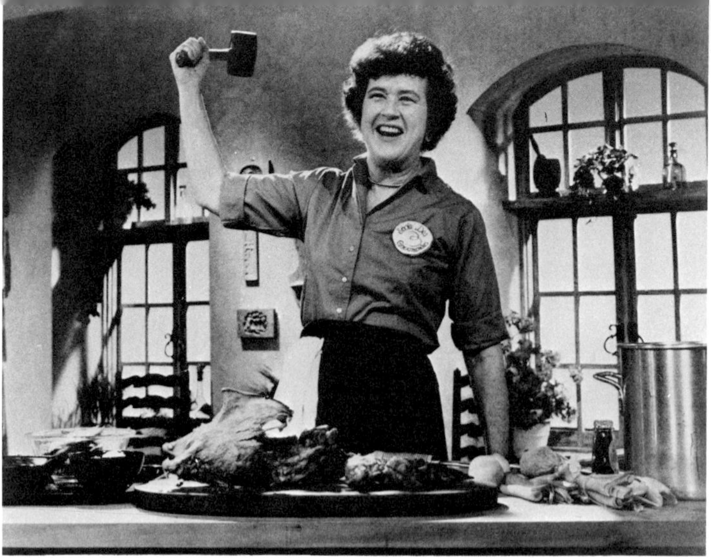

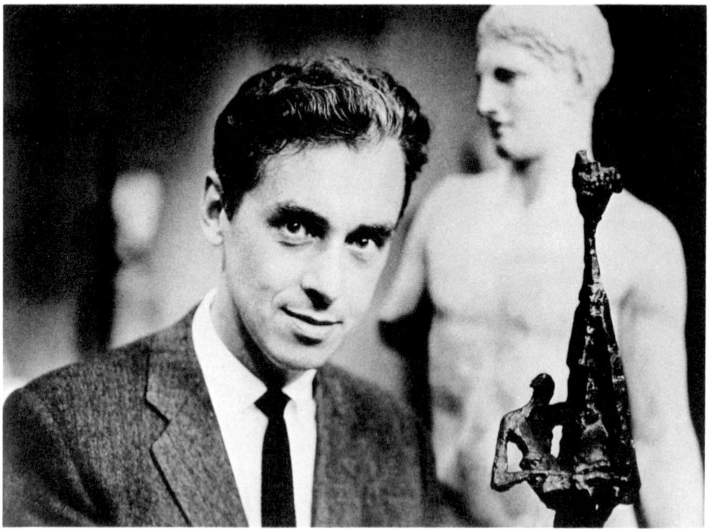

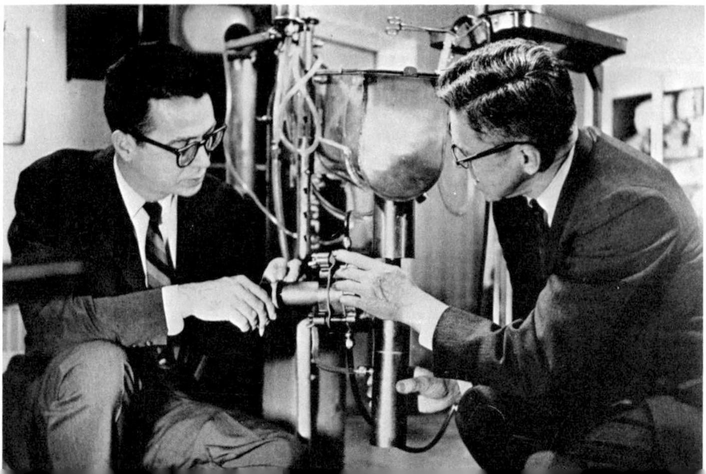

Educational Television

The Lowell Institute
Boston College
The Boston Symphony Orchestra
Boston University
Brandeis University
Harvard University
Massachusetts Institute of
 Technology

The Museum of Fine Arts
The Museum of Science
The New England Conservatory
 of Music
Northeastern University
Simmons College
Tufts University

No other broadcasting station in the world, it is believed, has a more impressive list of member institutions. Every one of them has contributed, and continues to contribute, through Channel 2 and WGBH-FM radio to the benefit and enjoyment of hundreds of thousands of persons a week. It is worth noting that half of the families with television in this region claim they watch Channel 2 occasionally, and that one third of the total can prove it by naming a program that they have seen within the past few days. Additional thousands are brought into the WGBH audience through WGBH-FM, which has been broadcasting since 1951.

Impressive as the results of this combination have been, the future holds far more in the way of community service from WGBH and its supporting institutions.

We are all quite accustomed to thinking about television as a mass medium. But we are not all aware of the growing use of television as a service to smaller special-interest groups within the community. This field is developing so rapidly that WGBH, with FCC approval, is now proceeding to

Channel 2's **Julia Child** stars weekly in *The French Chef,* the most popular program ever made for educational television. It is seen regularly on almost all the nation's 90-plus educational channels.

The Museum of Fine Arts is fully wired for television, and WGBH-TV produces two programs a week from the galleries. **Russell Connor,** opposite, stars on *Museum Open House,* while the other program, *Images,* consists entirely of works of art themselves with background commentary.

John Fitch, left, is the *M.I.T. Science Reporter* whose weekly program keeps the WGBH audience informed on the seething world of science. Here he examines a new heart-lung machine with inventor **D. Samuel Collins.**

build a new educational station for Boston that will operate on Channel 44 in the UHF band. Channel 44 will be devoted primarily to special-interest broadcasts, leaving more time on Channel 2 for broad cultural programming.

Already WGBH is moving into this field, making use of those scarcer and scarcer portions of the day that are not being taken up by in-school programs or by the regular evening schedule on Channel 2. Every Monday at mid-day and later in the evening, WGBH now airs a program for doctors. Its purpose is to make available to those who live far away from medical centers a convenient and effective method of keeping up with medical progress. Through the Tufts-New England Medical Center and the Postgraduate Medical Institute, and with funds from the Bingham Associates Fund and the U.S. Public Health Service, these programs are serving a real need for doctors.

WGBH is also one of the organizations that is cooperating with the new Center for Research and Development on Educational Differences at the Harvard Graduate School of Education. The station will make both closed and open circuit television available to the Center to put it in contact with schools, teachers and homes throughout New England.

The future of such special-purpose television is vast. WGBH has already received inquiries about programs for postgraduate and undergraduate training for nurses. We have had some preliminary conversations with businessmen interested in the application of television to in-plant training. There are similar opportunities in special-purpose television for government departments, for health and welfare agencies and for many other activities.

But there is no reason why special-purpose television should stop here. Television can and should become a major weapon in the nation's struggles against such things as technological unemployment, against youthful indifference, against voter apathy, and against that most shameful and tragic of all our problems, racial discrimination and the poverty with which it is so closely linked. Every major city in the nation has intensely difficult problems with poverty and Boston is no exception. Slums, and the conditions that create them, are America's national shame.

Why can't television be used to reach out to the people — and especially to the children — of the slums, and to show them the exits from poverty? U.S. Commissioner of Education Francis Keppel thinks it can. Just recently he said: "For years, we have told ourselves that these children of poverty are uneducable, or that their parents are not interested in what education could offer. Today's current events — from the civil rights movement to our experience in giving these children the best of education — now clearly re-

Educational Television

ject our prejudices. Television, I suggest, provides a means of augmenting the influence of the school in the slum and of involving the parent as well as the child in society's efforts to redress our failings of the past."

WGBH now has a new studio building, one of the finest in the country — educational or commercial. It is the gift of more than 50,000 New Englanders to replace the studios ruined by fire in 1961. This new building can and should be one of this city's and this region's major cultural resources. The building will be formally dedicated on May 1, just ten years since Channel 2 began broadcasting. And WGBH will dedicate itself on that day to the goal of making television a true servant of mankind. Television is too powerful a medium of communication to be devoted solely to entertainment and recreation, useful as these things may be.

Television has the power to do, or to help do, many of the things we all agree need doing in our society. With the continuing help of those institutions that have made so large a contribution already, WGBH will move ahead to a new era of service for the people of Boston, New England, and the nation.

HARTFORD N. GUNN, JR.
General Manager, WGBH

Educational Radio

Although all of the following stations are not educational, in that they are commercially sponsored, the programs are usually of good music.

WBCN 104.1 FM*

WBUR 90.9 FM
640 Commonwealth Avenue, Boston
program schedule published bi-monthly, free

WCRB 1330 AM, 102.5 FM
750 South Street, Waltham
program schedule published monthly
$3.50 yearly, $2.50 school year

WERS 88.9 FM
130 Beacon Street, Boston
program schedule published bi-monthly, free

WGBH 89.7 FM
program schedule for TV and FM
published monthly
$10.00 donation

WHRB 95.3 FM*

WXHR 96.9 FM, **WTAO** 740 AM*

*program schedules listed in *Good Listening*

The Cultural Resources of Boston

Daytime Stargazing in the Charles Hayden Planetarium at the Museum of Science, where the American-made Korkosz projector gives an amazingly realistic depiction of nighttime skies past, present, and future.

11 Science Museums

Taken together, the Greater Boston museums dedicated to the sciences and industry are, like our revitalized center city, a commingling of changelessness and change. In them, the past rubs elbows with the present to give lustre to the promises of the future.

Fortunate in being located in an area with a great cultural heritage and surrounded with probably the greatest resource of scientific advice and know-how on earth, they are singularly equipped to present the exciting true story of our planet and what is happening on it to their millions of visitors.

Some, notably the great University museums at Harvard, are research and study museums, primarily for the serious student.

The great majority of the men, women, and children who visit the others will probably never be scientists, but they will be better lawyers, businessmen, clergymen, scoutmasters, parents, citizens, because of the glimpses at the wonders of nature and the use man has made of them that are spread out in fascinating three-dimension before their eyes. And for a certain few youngsters, these museums will generate the first spark of interest that eventually will lead to a lifetime career.

Among all the various kinds of informal learning, museums have a unique appeal. Their specialty is objects — real, material things that give life to words. Often these objects are original evidences of the past. Again, they may be models that make little things big and big things little.

Words have a slippery way of changing meaning when they reach the mind. Objects dress words with reality. They give substance to photographs and films. Often, modern museums, in Boston as elsewhere, build programs that may include photographs, films, lectures, and demonstrations around these objects . . . or they may activate them . . . or invite the audience to activate them. But always the take-off point is the object itself.

One of these days three astronauts are going to climb into an Apollo capsule, atop a 360-foot-tall Saturn V rocket, for an epochal journey to the moon. When they do, a few hundred thousand men, women, and children are going to recall that they saw manikin doubles of these spacemen in a full-scale model of the capsule at Boston's **Museum of Science,** at least five years before this thrilling journey.

They will also likely recall a series of scale models of rockets, beginning with the early Goddard and ending with the Saturn, that briefly but graphically illustrated the tremendous strides made in this science in a few short years.

Again, many of them may remember a program in the Museum's Hayden

The Cultural Resources of Boston

Planetarium that took them on a breathtakingly realistic depiction of this same lunar trip.

The destination of these astronauts will also remind some of these visitors that they stood in the Planetarium lobby before a giant mural of a lunar crater which was as scientifically correct as it could be, from what was known at the time, of the topography of the moon. Undoubtedly these visitors, conjuring up the Museum mural, will be making comparisons when those astronauts return.

So will the staff of the Museum of Science, you can be sure of that! And if changes are needed to conform with reality, they will be made on the spot.

Updating its ever-growing collection of exhibits on science, industry, natural history, man and civilization, medicine, and astronomy goes on constantly at the Museum of Science. This museum, an outgrowth of one of the earliest in the country, the New England Museum of Natural History, is a proponent of the activated type of exhibit, with, whenever possible, audience participation. Its 400,000 visitors annually are invited to watch the earth spin, listen to the talking Transparent Woman, play tick-tac-toe with a computer, weigh themselves on the moon, see liquid air, meet a live Great Horned Owl, hear a heartbeat, and steer a ship. It is the kind of museum that offers something for everyone, no matter what the age or interest.

Beckoning woodland paths and friendly live animals are among the tempting lures that lead young people to the **Blue Hills Trailside Museum** in Milton.

Trailside is a charming natural history museum with small birds and animals, native to the Blue Hills, that are regularly taken out and shown to visitors; lifelike models and live specimens of plants of the area; and examples of a geological past that goes back to the Ice Age. Trailside is also a series of nature trails, with instructor guides, that cut through beautiful wooded hills bountifully supplied with flora and fauna.

The kind of vital, close contact with nature found at this museum can be a lasting experience for the young and impressionable, enriching their entire lives.

Similar personal introductions to the wonders of nature are open to city youngsters at the **Children's Museum** in the Jamaica Plain section of Boston.

For many years this popular museum has been conducting nature walks

Children's Museum. Children find out what is inside things found around the house. They can operate the see-through washing machine, turn on the light bulb with a rheostat, see a cut-away toilet, inside of a mattress, etc.

Following pathway to nature's wonders in backyard of **Blue Hills Trailside Museum**, in Milton.

125

around Jamaica Pond and other nearby areas of the city's green belt — making abundantly clear that living in the City does not mean a child must forego the pleasures of close acquaintance with outdoor life. In the museum itself they learn more about the nature around them with exhibits, clubs, and live animals.

This museum also makes a real effort in its exhibits and program to awaken an awareness of the customs of other lands and times. And recently it opened a thoroughly intriguing new section called, "What's Inside." Here, youngsters discover answers to such questions as what makes movies move, what's inside a drop of pond water, and what makes home appliances work. Most thrilling of all is a part of a city street with a manhole to be explored.

The five so-called **Harvard University museums,** are, as I said before, primarily research museums. Yet, 120,000 nonstudent visitors a year make their way to one of the smallest, the Botanical Museum, to view the famous Ware Collection of Glass Flowers, beautiful and unique models made in Germany by Leopold and Rudolph Blaschka.

And on rainy week-ends parents and their children flock to the others: the Peabody Museum of American Archaeology and Ethnology, the Mineralogical and Geological Museums, and especially the Museum of Comparative Zoology, founded by Louis Agassiz in 1859. This first of America's great university museums grew out of the brilliant scientist's personal collections. A longtime Harvard professor, he was an advocate of the laboratory method of scientific study, rather than the textbook. To prove his point he would remind his students that because Aristotle said the mayfly had four legs it was so taught for two millenia. But if you looked at the fly itself you would discover that there are actually six!

While only a small part of the Museum of Comparative Zoology is presented to public view, this includes the most spectacular exhibits. Visitors today can follow Agassiz' teachings by studying some of the rare examples of our prehistoric past displayed here — such as the 42-foot-long skeleton of what is believed to be the largest marine reptile that ever lived. This is the world's only mounted specimen of Kronosaurus, which swam the seas about 120 million years ago, and became extinct about the same time as the dinosaurs.

From prehistoric to historic past is but a matter of a few miles for Greater Boston museum-goers.

The beginning of America's industrial development — actually the birth

Science Museums

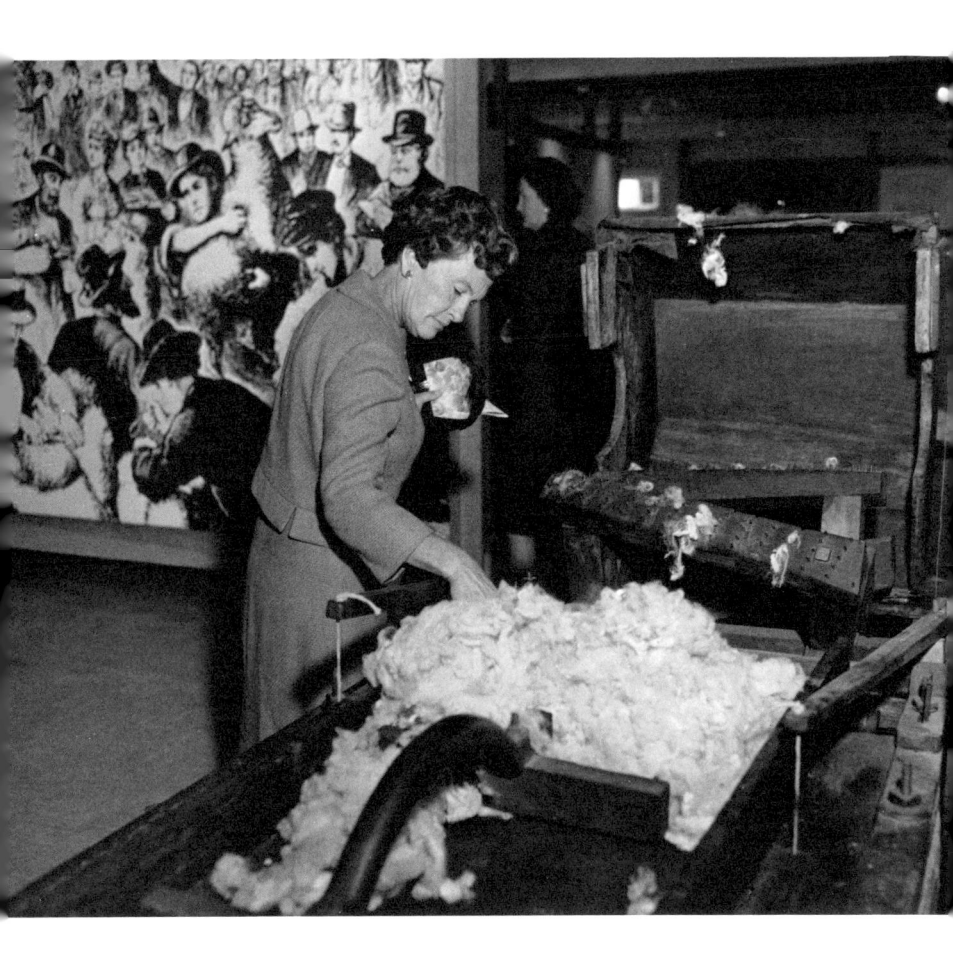

of our mighty iron and steel industry — took place just 10 miles north of Boston, in Saugus, where today you can see an authentic recreation of the original **Saugus Ironworks.**

As you tour this restoration, with its blast furnace, forge, rolling and slitting mill, warehouse, and wharf, you will surely marvel at the temerity and technological know-how of the men who built this enterprise in the wilderness of the Massachusetts Bay Colony only 26 years after the arrival of the Pilgrims.

The Saugus Ironworks Restoration has been as faithfully created as

Merrimack Valley Textile Museum.
Picking wool is one of the earliest of several processes necessary to convert sheep's fleece into a man's coat. This machine is from the early 19th century.

humanly possible by the iron and steel industry and the First Iron Works Association, Inc.

A later period in our American history, the Industrial Revolution, brought great and sudden changes locally, especially in cloth making, which before 1800 was widely practiced in the homes. **The Merrimack Valley Textile Museum** in North Andover serves as a center for the study of the role of wool manufacturing in American history, and contains exhibits emphasizing the transition from handicraft to factory production.

For memorabilia of our maritime past, when Boston and Salem Clippers sailed to all corners of the earth, there is the **Peabody Museum** in Salem, the "museum built by navigators." Originally begun to house the curiosities from exotic lands brought back by captains and supercargo of the East India Marine Society, it now has three main classes of collections: maritime history, ethnology, and the natural history of Essex County.

Further opportunities for nautical exploration are available in Cambridge, at the **Francis Hart Nautical Museum** in the School of Naval Architecture and Marine Engineering at the Massachusetts Institute of Technology.

The "Museum of Motoring Progress" or **Antique Auto Museum** at Larz Anderson Park in Brookline dramatizes another, more general, form of transportation. The first steam automobile, that lumbered through the streets in 1866 — and still works, an 1899 Winton, an early Electromobile, and many more antique cars and carriages highlight the evolution of transportation from about 1850 to the late 1920's in this growing museum, where exhibits are changed periodically.

To sum up. Separately, each of these museums has its own particular appeal and power to stir the imagination and enlighten the mind. Together, with all their exhibits and collections — some of them the best and the most extensive to be found anywhere — they can only begin to show us the vast magnitude and complexity of our world. The world itself is the only museum that can do that!

BRADFORD WASHBURN
Director
Museum of Science, Boston

Science Museums

Museums of Science and Industry in the Greater Boston area:

Antique Auto Museum of Massachusetts
(Museum of Motoring Progress)
Larz Anderson Park, 15 Newton St., Brookline
Open Tues. through Sun., 1-5 p.m.
Closed Mon.
Admission — 25¢ children; 50¢ adults

Blue Hills Trailside Museum
(Metropolitan District Commission)
1904 Canton Ave., Milton
Open Oct. through April, Thurs. through Sat., 10 a.m.-5 p.m.; Sun., 1-5 p.m.
Open May through Sept., Tues. through Sat., 10 a.m.-5 p.m.; Sun., 1-5 p.m.
Admission 10¢ children under 12; 25¢ age 12 and over

Children's Museum
60 Burroughs St., Jamaica Plain
Open Tues. through Sat., 9 a.m.-5 p.m.; Sun., 1-5 p.m. Closed Mon.
Admission 25¢ for children and adults

Francis Hart Nautical Museum
(Massachusetts Institute of Technology)
School of Naval Architecture and Marine Engineering, Mass. Ave., Cambridge
Open every day and evening
Admission free

Harvard University Museums
Oxford St., Cambridge
Open weekdays 9 a.m.-4:30 p.m.; Sundays, 1-4:30 p.m.
Admission free except Botanical Museum (glass flowers) 25¢

Museum of Science and Hayden Planetarium
Science Park, Boston
Open Tues. through Sat., 10 a.m.-5 p.m.; Fri. night to 10; Sun., 1-5 p.m.; Closed Mon.
Planetarium star showings Tues. through Fri., 11 a.m. and 3 p.m.; Fri. night at 8; Sat., 11 a.m., 1:45, 3 p.m.; Sun., 1:45, 3, 4:15 p.m.
Admission to Museum 25¢ children under 12; 50¢ 12 through 16 yrs.; $1 adults, Planetarium 50¢ additional for everyone.

Merrimack Valley Textile Museum
Massachusetts Ave., North Andover
Open Tues. through Sat., 10 a.m.-4 p.m.; Sun., 1-5 p.m. Closed Mon.
Admission free

Peabody Museum
161 Essex St., Salem
Open daily 9 a.m.-5 p.m.; Sun. and holidays, 2-5 p.m. (except 4 p.m. closing Nov. 1 to Mar. 1)
Admission free

Saugus Ironworks Restoration
Central St., Saugus
Open May 15 through Oct. 15 daily except Sun., 9 a.m.-4 p.m.
Admission to Ironmaster's House and Ironworks 50¢ children; $1 adults; To Ironworks only, 25¢ children

The Children's Museum, boys emerging from the man-hole onto the paved "street". The man-hole is fitted with cut-away telephone cables, etc.

De Cordova Museum, during a painting class

12　For Children

This listing does not preclude children's interest in other material in the book, but is a gathering of information for convenience. Detailed ticket information and schedules of programs are available from the institutions upon request. Institutions are listed **by location,** proceeding outward from Boston. They are grouped according to their principal areas of concern, described in each entry.

Children's Museum
60 Burroughs Street, Jamaica Plain.
524-1551
Tuesday – Saturday, 9 to 5; Sunday, 1 to 5.
Natural History, Social Sciences, Dolls and Doll Houses
25¢ or membership rates available
Special programs for groups
Winter Discovery Workshops
Vacation Week Programs, Story Hours
Saturday Children's Theater
Nature Walks

Museum of Science
on Charles River Dam Bridge, Boston.
742-1410
Tuesday – Saturday, 10 to 5;
Friday to 10, Sunday, 1 to 5.
Science, Natural History, Man, Medicine
Astronomy. Demonstrations with live animals and talking transparent woman
25¢ children under 12, 50¢ ages 12 to 16
Adults $1.00
Charles Hayden Planetarium, 45 minute showings with lecture. 50¢ additional

Blue Hills Trailside Museum
1904 Canton Avenue, Milton. 333-0690
Winter: Thursday – Saturday, 10 to 5; Sunday, 1 to 5.
Summer: Tuesday – Saturday, 10 to 5; Sunday, 1 to 5.
Natural History exhibitions, walks, talks
10¢ children under 12, others 25¢

Drumlin Farm Wildlife Sanctuary
Massachusetts Audubon Society
5 Great Road, Lincoln. 259-9500
Monday – Sunday, 9 to 5.
Educational Farm group school tours, Monday – Friday

Saturday, Sunday at 3, Nature programs
$1.00 parking charge or membership rates available

Perkins School for the Blind Museum
175 North Beacon Street, Watertown.
924-3434
By appointment Monday – Friday, 9 to 4

Children's Art Centre Inc.
36 Rutland Street, Boston. 536-9666
Monday – Friday, 9 to 5;
Saturday, 9 to 11:30.
Daily classes in various media
Exhibitions of children's work and Contemporary Art

Museum of Fine Arts
465 Huntington Avenue, Boston.
367-9300
The Children's Room
Gallery talk and related creative work
Tuesday Grades 1 & 2, 3 to 4:30
Wednesday Grades 3 & 4, 3 to 4:30
Friday Grades 5 & 6, 3 to 4:30
Saturday Grades 1–6 (for those unable to attend during week), 10:15 to 11:45 or 1:30 to 3:00
Free ticket 15 minutes before class
Gallery talk for children and parents last Sunday of the month, 2:00

Cambridge Art Center
31 Newtowne Court, Cambridge.
864-3840
During school year, Monday – Saturday
Classes in various media

Project Inc.
141 Huron Avenue, Cambridge. 491-0187
During school year, Monday – Saturday
Classes in creative art projects, ages 4 to 12

The Cultural Resources of Boston

Charles River Art Center
1361 South Street, Needham. 444-1393
Saturday classes in drawing, painting and crafts

De Cordova Museum
Sandy Pond Road, Lincoln. 259-8355
During school year, Tuesday – Saturday
Classes in Art, Dance, Dramatics
Summer: intensive art program, grades 3 to 7, 4 mornings a week, six weeks
Concert series at Lexington High School

Boston Children's Theater
263 Commonwealth Avenue, Boston. 536-3324
October – May, 5 productions, 3–5 weeks each held at New England Life Hall
July – August, Stagemobile tours in greater Boston
Creative dramatics classes

Charles Playhouse
Musical Theater for Children
76 Warrenton Street, Boston. 338-9393
September – May, Thursday at 3:30;
Saturday at 11 and 2
Daily 11 and 2 during school vacations

Children's Concerts
Symphony Hall, Boston. 266-1492
November, January, March
three concerts each month
Saturday mornings

Children's Esplanade Concerts
During the Esplanade season

Greater Boston Youth Symphony Orchestra
(composed of high school juniors and seniors)
and
Greater Boston Youth Junior Symphony Orchestra
(composed of students, seventh grade to sophomore)
B.U. School of Fine and Applied Arts, Boston. 262-4300 ext. 8220
Concerts given during the year at Symphony and Jordan Halls, schools

Young Audiences
116 Newbury Street, Boston. 266-0322
Concerts given in the greater Boston area schools and institutions

Children's Concert Series
Club 47, 47 Palmer Street, Cambridge. 864-3266
September – May, Saturday at 2
Concerts, folk music, dance and story telling programs

The Freedom Trail
Walking tour
featuring 15 of the nation's most famous historical sites. The Trail covers about 1½ miles. In a circular route. Starting with Park Street Church.

Seasonal Events for Children

Children's Book Fair
held at New England Life Hall, 225 Clarendon Street
November (Children's Book Week)
Display of pre-school through teen-ager books
Sponsored by the Boston Herald Traveler
Boston Public Library
Children's Book Council
Massachusetts Department of Education

Massachusetts Scholastic Art Awards Exhibition
held at Boston University, School of Fine and Applied Arts
855 Commonwealth Avenue. 262-4300
February
Selected work by Massachusetts school children
Sponsored by the Boston Globe

Massachusetts State Science Fair
held at Rockwell Cage, Massachusetts Institute of Technology
May
Science displays and demonstrations by Massachusetts high school students
Sponsored by the Boston Globe

Books and Background

ABOUT BOSTON
Sight, Sound, Flavor & Inflection
David McCord
Little, Brown & Company,
Boston, Mass., 1964

ARCHITECTURAL FORUM
Special Issue: Boston
June 1964

BOOK OF BOSTON
Vol. I The Colonial Period 1960
Vol. II The Federal Period 1961
Vol. III The Victorian Period 1964
Marjorie Drake Ross
Hastings House Publishers, Inc.,
New York

BOSTON ARCHITECTURE 1637-1954
Henry-Russell Hitchcock
Reinhold Publishing Corp.,
New York, 1954

BOSTON: Portrait of a City
Text by Walter Muir Whitehill,
Photographs by Katharine Knowles
Barre Publishing Co., Inc.,
Barre, Mass., 1964

BOSTON a topographical history
Walter Muir Whitehill
Harvard University Press,
Cambridge, Mass., 1959

BOSTON WAYS, high, by and folk
George F. Weston
Beacon Press, Boston, Mass., 1957

BULFINCH'S BOSTON, 1787-1817
Harold and James Kirker
Oxford University Press, New York, 1964

FREEDOM TRAIL, Guide to
John Hancock Mutual Life Insurance
Company
available at above or Freedom Trail
Shrines, free

**THE MASSACHUSETTS STATE
HOUSE,** A New Guide
Sinclair H. Hitchings &
Catherine H. Farlow
John Hancock Mutual Life Insurance
Company 1964
available at the State House, $1.00

THE FOGG ART MUSEUM
A Survey of the Collections
Harvard University,
Cambridge, Mass., 1964
$2.00

GUIDE TO THE COLLECTION
Isabella Stewart Gardner Museum
$.75

ILLUSTRATED HANDBOOK
Museum of Fine Arts 1964
$2.00 paper, $7.00 cloth bound

JEWETT ARTS CENTER,
Catalogue of the Collection
Curtis H. Shell & John McAndrew
Wellesley College 1958 $1.50

**GUIDE TO THE ART MUSEUMS OF
NEW ENGLAND**
Lane S. Faison, Jr.
Harcourt, Brace & World, Inc.,
New York, 1958

**NEW ENGLAND MUSEUMS AND
HISTORIC HOUSES**
New England Council
Museum of Fine Arts
Society for the Preservation of
New England Antiquities
available at M.F.A. & S.P.N.E.A.
annually, free

NORTHEASTERN TOUR BOOK
American Automobile Association 1964
available to A.A.A. members

**BOSTON CENTER FOR
ADULT EDUCATION**
5 Commonwealth Avenue
quarterly

**CAMBRIDGE CENTER FOR
ADULT EDUCATION**
42 Brattle Street
quarterly

EDUCATIONAL OPPORTUNITIES of
Greater Boston for Adults
Educational Exchange of Greater Boston
18 Brattle Street, Cambridge
annually in August, $2.50

BOSTON Magazine
Greater Boston Chamber of Commerce
125 High Street, Boston
monthly, $.50 newsstands, $5.00 yearly

GOOD LISTENING
270 Summer Street, Boston
monthly, $.35 newsstands, $3.50 yearly

NUCLEUS
Northeastern University
Office of Publications
September, November, January, March
nominal charge

PANORAMA Magazine
270 Summer Street, Boston
monthly, $.35 newsstands, $4.00 yearly

**Institutional Calendars of Events
Open to the Public**

BOSTON COLLEGE
Secretary of the University
monthly, free

**BOSTON CONSERVATORY OF
MUSIC**
monthly, free

BOSTON PUBLIC LIBRARY NEWS
monthly, free

BOSTON UNIVERSITY
School of Fine and Applied Arts
monthly

BRANDEIS UNIVERSITY
Office of Public Affairs
monthly, free

CHILDREN'S MUSEUM
quarterly, with membership,
$1.00 Junior minimum

EMERSON COLLEGE
Office of Theater Arts
annually, free

HARVARD UNIVERSITY GAZETTE
8 Everett Street
weekly, $1.50 term, $3.00 school year

HEBREW TEACHERS COLLEGE
bi-monthly, free

**INTERNATIONAL STUDENT
ASSOCIATION**
for full time students only
bi-monthly, free

LOWELL INSTITUTE
Curator of Lowell Institute
Boston Public Library
annually, fall, free

**MASSACHUSETTS INSTITUTE OF
TECHNOLOGY**
Office of Public Relations
weekly, September – June
$1.50 term, $3.00 yearly, payable to
W. A. Hokanson

MUSEUM OF FINE ARTS
Treasurer's Office
monthly, October – June
$1.50 yearly

**NEW ENGLAND CONSERVATORY
OF MUSIC**
Office of Public Relations
monthly, September – May, free

PINE MANOR JUNIOR COLLEGE
Office of Public Relations
each semester, free

TUFTS UNIVERSITY
Calendar Office
weekly, free

WELLESLEY COLLEGE
Information Center
weekly, September – May, $1.00

Information about lectures can also be
obtained from:

BOSTON ARCHITECTURAL CENTER
320 Newbury Street. 536-7146

FORD HALL FORUM
80 Boylston Street. 426-0257